ANIMAL STORIES

Animal Stories

by

Rudyard Kipling

Dales Large Print Books
Long Preston, North Yorkshire,
BD23 4ND, England.

British Library Cataloguing in Publication Data.

Kipling, Rudyard
    Animal stories.

    A catalogue record of this book is
    available from the British Library

    ISBN   1-84262-327-3 pbk

Cover illustration by arrangement with House of Stratus

Published in Large Print 2004 by arrangement with
House of Stratus

Dales Large Print is an imprint of Library Magna Books Ltd.

Printed and bound in Great Britain by
T.J. (International) Ltd., Cornwall, PL28 8RW

CONTENTS

THE CAMEL'S HUMP

The Camel's hump is an ugly lump
Which well you may see at the Zoo;
But uglier yet is the Hump we get
From having too little to do.

Kiddies and grown-ups too-oo-oo,
If we haven't enough to do-oo-oo,
We get the Hump–
Cameelious Hump–
The Hump that is black and blue!

We climb out of bed with a frouzly head
And a snarly-yarly voice.
We shiver and scowl and we grunt and we
   growl
At our bath and our boots and our toys;

And there ought to be a corner for me
(And I know there is one for you)
When we get the Hump–
Cameelious Hump–
The Hump that is black and blue!

The cure for this ill is not to sit still,
Or frowst with a book by the fire;
But to take a large hoe and a shovel also,

11

And dig till you gently perspire;

And then you will find that the sun and
  the wind,
And the Djinn of the Garden too,
Have lifted the Hump–
That horrible Hump–
The Hump that is black and blue!

I get it as well as you-oo-oo
If I haven't enough to do-oo-oo!
We all get Hump–
Cameelious Hump–
Kiddies and grown-ups too!

THE CAT THAT
WALKED BY HIMSELF

Hear and attend and listen; for this befell and behappened and became and was, O my Best Beloved, when the Tame animals were wild. The Dog was wild, and the Horse was wild, and the Cow was wild, and the Sheep was wild, and the Pig was wild – as wild as wild could be – and they walked in the Wet Wild Woods by their wild lones. But the wildest of all the wild animals was the Cat. He walked by himself, and all places were alike to him.

Of course the Man was wild too. He was dreadfully wild. He didn't even begin to be tame till he met the Woman, and she told him that she did not like living in his wild ways. She picked out a nice dry Cave, instead of a heap of wet leaves, to lie down in; and she strewed clean sand on the floor; and she lit a nice fire of wood at the back of the Cave; and she hung a dried wildhorse skin, tail-down, across the opening of the Cave; and she said, 'Wipe your feet, dear, when you come in, and now we'll keep house.'

That night, Best Beloved, they ate wild

sheep roasted on the hot stones, and flavoured with wild garlic and wild pepper; and wild duck stuffed with wild rice and wild fenugreek and wild coriander; and marrow-bones of wild oxen; and wild cherries, and wild grenadillas. Then the Man went to sleep in front of the fire ever so happy; but the Woman sat up, combing her hair. She took the bone of the shoulder of mutton – the big flat blade-bone – and she looked at the wonderful marks on it, and she threw more wood on the fire, and she made a Magic. She made the First Singing Magic in the world.

Out in the Wet Wild Woods all the wild animals gathered together where they could see the light of the fire a long way off, and they wondered what it meant.

Then Wild Horse stamped with his wild foot and said, 'O my Friends and O my Enemies, why have the Man and the Woman made that great light in that great Cave, and what harm will it do us?'

Wild Dog lifted up his wild nose and smelled the smell of the roast mutton, and said, 'I will go up and see and look, and say; for I think it is good. Cat, come with me.'

'Nenni!' said the Cat. 'I am the Cat who walks by himself, and all places are alike to me. I will not come.'

'Then we can never be friends again,' said Wild Dog, and he trotted off to the Cave.

But when he had gone a little way the Cat said to himself, 'All places are alike to me. Why should I not go too and see and look and come away at my own liking?' So he slipped after Wild Dog softly, very softly, and hid himself where he could hear everything.

When Wild Dog reached the mouth of the Cave he lifted up the dried horse-skin with his nose and sniffed the beautiful smell of the roast mutton, and the Woman, looking at the blade-bone, heard him, and laughed, and said, 'Here comes the first. Wild Thing out of the Wild Woods, what do you want?'

Wild Dog said, 'O my Enemy and Wife of my Enemy, what is this that smells so good in the Wild Woods?'

Then the Woman picked up a roasted mutton-bone and threw it to Wild Dog, and said, 'Wild Thing out of the Wild Woods, taste and try.' Wild Dog gnawed the bone, and it was more delicious than anything he had ever tasted, and he said, 'O my Enemy and Wife of my Enemy, give me another.'

The Woman said, 'Wild Thing out of the Wild Woods, help my Man to hunt through the day and guard this Cave at night, and I will give you as many roast bones as you need.'

'Ah!' said the Cat, listening. 'This is a very wise Woman, but she is not so wise as I am.'

Wild Dog crawled into the Cave and laid

his head on the Woman's lap, and said, 'O my Friend and Wife of my Friend, I will help your Man to hunt through the day, and at night I will guard your Cave.'

'Ah!' said the Cat, listening. 'That is a very foolish Dog.' And he went back through the Wet Wild Woods waving his wild tail, and walking by his wild lone. But he never told anybody.

When the Man waked up he said, 'What is Wild Dog doing here?' And the Woman said, 'His name is not Wild Dog any more, but the First Friend, because he will be our friend for always and always and always. Take him with you when you go hunting.'

Next night the Woman cut great green armfuls of fresh grass from the water-meadows, and dried it before the fire, so that it smelt like new-mown hay, and she sat at the mouth of the Cave and plaited a halter out of horse-hide, and she looked at the shoulder-of-mutton bone – at the big broad blade-bone – and she made a Magic. She made the Second Singing Magic in the world.

Out in the Wild Woods all the wild animals wondered what had happened to Wild Dog, and at last Wild Horse stamped with his foot and said, 'I will go and see and say why Wild Dog has not returned. Cat, come with me.'

'Nenni!' said the Cat. 'I am the Cat who walks by himself, and all places are alike to me. I will not come.' But all the same he followed Wild Horse softly, very softly, and hid himself where he could hear everything.

When the Woman heard Wild Horse tripping and stumbling on his long mane, she laughed and said, 'Here comes the second. Wild Thing Out of the Wild Woods, what do you want?'

Wild Horse said, 'O my Enemy and Wife of my Enemy, where is Wild Dog?'

The Woman laughed, and picked up the blade-bone and looked at it, and said, 'Wild Thing out of the Wild Woods, you did not come here for Wild Dog, but for the sake of this good grass.'

And Wild Horse, tripping and stumbling on his long mane, said, 'That is true; give it me to eat.'

The Woman said, 'Wild Thing out of the Wild Woods, bend your wild head and wear what I give you, and you shall eat the wonderful grass three times a day.'

'Ah!' said the Cat, listening. 'This is a clever Woman, but she is not so clever as I am.'

Wild Horse bent his wild head, and the Woman slipped the plaited-hide halter over it, and Wild Horse breathed on the Woman's feet and said, 'O my Mistress, and Wife of my Master, I will be your servant for the sake of the wonderful grass.'

'Ah!' said the Cat, listening. 'That is a very

17

foolish Horse.' And he went back through the Wet Wild Woods, waving his wild tail and walking by his wild lone. But he never told anybody.

When the Man and the Dog came back from hunting, the Man said, 'What is Wild Horse doing here?' And the Woman said, 'His name is not Wild Horse any more, but the First Servant, because he will carry us from place to place for always and always and always. Ride on his back when you go hunting.'

Next day, holding her wild head high that her wild horns should not catch in the wild trees, Wild Cow came up to the Cave, and the Cat followed, and hid himself just the same as before; and every thing happened just the same as before; and the Cat said the same things as before; and when Wild Cow had promised to give her milk to the Woman every day in exchange for the wonderful grass, the Cat went back through the Wet Wild Woods waving his wild tail and walking by his wild lone, just the same as before. But he never told anybody. And when the Man and the Horse and the Dog came home from hunting and asked the same questions same as before, the Woman said, 'Her name is not Wild Cow any more, but the Giver of Good Food. She will give us the warm white milk for always and always and always, and I will take care of her while you and the

First Friend and the First Servant go hunting.'

Next day the Cat waited to see if any other Wild Thing would go up to the Cave, but no one moved in the Wet Wild Woods, so the Cat walked there by himself; and he saw the Woman milking the Cow, and he saw the light of the fire in the Cave, and he smelt the smell of the warm white milk.

Cat said, 'O my Enemy and Wife of my Enemy, where did Wild Cow go?'

The Woman laughed and said, 'Wild Thing out of the Wild Woods, go back to the Woods again, for I have braided up my hair, and I have put away the magic blade-bone, and we have no more need of either friends or servants in our Cave.'

Cat said, 'I am not a friend, and I am not a servant. I am the Cat who walks by himself, and I wish to come into your Cave.'

Woman said, 'Then why did you not come with First Friend on the first night?'

Cat grew very angry and said, 'Has Wild Dog told tales of me?'

Then the Woman laughed and said, 'You are the Cat who walks by himself, and all places are alike to you. You are neither a friend nor a servant. You have said it yourself. Go away and walk by yourself in all places alike.'

Then Cat pretended to be sorry and said, 'Must I never come into the Cave? Must I never sit by the warm fire? Must I never drink the warm white milk? You are very wise and very beautiful. You should not be cruel even to a Cat.'

Woman said, 'I knew I was wise, but I did not know I was beautiful. So I will make a bargain with you. If ever I say one word in your praise, you may come into the Cave.'

'And if you say two words in my praise?' said the Cat.

'I never shall,' said the Woman, 'but if I say two words in your praise, you may sit by the fire in the Cave.'

'And if you say three words?' said the Cat.

'I never shall,' said the Woman, 'but if I say three words in your praise, you may drink the warm white milk three times a day for always and always and always.'

Then the Cat arched his back and said, 'Now let the Curtain at the mouth of the Cave, and the Fire at the back of the Cave, and the Milk-pots that stand beside the Fire, remember what my Enemy and the Wife of my Enemy has said.' And he went away through the Wet Wild Woods waving his wild tail and walking by his wild lone.

That night when the Man and the Horse and the Dog came home from hunting, the Woman did not tell them of the bargain that she had made with the Cat, because she was afraid that they might not like it.

Cat went far and far away and hid himself

in the Wet Wild Woods by his wild lone for a long time till the Woman forgot all about him. Only the Bat – the little upside-down Bat – that hung inside the Cave knew where Cat hid; and every evening Bat would fly to Cat with news of what was happening.

One evening Bat said, 'There is a Baby in the Cave. He is new and pink and fat and small, and the Woman is very fond of him.'

'Ah,' said the Cat, listening, 'but what is the Baby fond of?'

'He is fond of things that are soft and tickle,' said the Bat. 'He is fond of warm things to hold in his arms when he goes to sleep. He is fond of being played with. He is fond of all those things.'

'Ah,' said the Cat, listening, 'then my time has come.'

Next night Cat walked through the Wet Wild Woods and hid very near the Cave till morning-time, and Man and Dog and Horse went hunting. The Woman was busy cooking that morning, and the Baby cried and interrupted. So she carried him outside the Cave and gave him a handful of pebbles to play with. But still the Baby cried.

Then the Cat put out his paddy paw and patted the Baby on the cheek, and it cooed; and the Cat rubbed against its fat knees and tickled it under its fat chin with his tail. And the Baby laughed; and the Woman heard him and smiled.

Then the Bat – the little upside-down Bat – that hung in the mouth of the Cave said, 'O my Hostess and Wife of my Host and Mother of my Host's Son, a Wild Thing from the Wild Woods is most beautifully playing with your Baby.'

'A blessing on that Wild Thing whoever he may be,' said the Woman, straightening her back, 'for I was a busy woman this morning and he has done me a service.'

That very minute and second, Best Beloved, the dried horseskin Curtain that was stretched tail-down at the mouth of the Cave fell down – *woosh!* – because it remembered the bargain she had made with the Cat; and when the Woman went to pick it up – lo and behold – the Cat was sitting quite comfy inside the Cave.

'O my Enemy and Wife of my Enemy and Mother of my Enemy,' said the Cat, 'it is I: for you have spoken a word in my praise, and now I can sit within the Cave for always and always and always. But still I am the Cat who walks by himself, and all places are alike to me.'

The Woman was very angry, and shut her lips tight and took up her spinning-wheel and began to spin.

But the Baby cried because the Cat had gone away, and the Woman could not hush it, for it struggled and kicked and grew black in the face.

'O my Enemy and Wife of my Enemy and Mother of my Enemy,' said the Cat, 'take a strand of the thread that you are spinning and tie it to your spinning-whorl and drag it along the floor, and I will show you a Magic that shall make your Baby laugh as loudly as he is now crying.'

'I will do so,' said the Woman, 'because I am at my wits' end; but I will not thank you for it.'

She tied the thread to the little clay spindle-whorl and drew it across the floor, and the Cat ran after it and patted it with his paws and rolled head over heels, and tossed it backward over his shoulder and chased it between his hind-legs and pretended to lose it and pounced down upon it again, till the Baby laughed as loudly as it had been crying, and scrambled after the Cat and frolicked all over the Cave till it grew tired and settled down to sleep with the Cat in its arms.

'Now,' said Cat, 'I will sing the Baby a song that shall keep him asleep for an hour.' And he began to purr, loud and low, low and loud, till the Baby fell fast asleep. The Woman smiled as she looked down upon the two of them, and said, 'That was wonderfully done. No question but you are very clever, O Cat.'

That very minute and second, Best Beloved, the smoke of the Fire at the back of the Cave came down in clouds from the roof – *puff* – because it remembered the bargain she had made with the Cat; and when it had cleared away – lo and behold! – the Cat was sitting quite comfy close to the fire.

'O my Enemy and Wife of my Enemy and Mother of my Enemy,' said the Cat, 'it is I: for you have spoken a second word in my praise, and now I can sit by the warm fire at the back of the Cave for always and always and always. But still I am the Cat who walks by himself, and all places are alike to me.'

Then the Woman was very very angry, and let down her hair and put more wood on the fire and brought out the broad blade-bone of the shoulder of mutton and began to make a Magic that should prevent her from saying a third word in praise of the Cat. It was not a Singing Magic, Best Beloved, it was a Still Magic; and by and by the Cave grew so still that a little wee-wee mouse crept out of a corner and ran across the floor.

'O my Enemy and Wife of my Enemy and Mother of my Enemy,' said the Cat, 'is that little mouse part of your Magic?'

'Ouh! Chee! No indeed!' said the Woman, and she dropped the blade-bone and jumped upon the footstool in front of the fire and braided up her hair very quick for fear that the mouse should run up it.

'Ah,' said the Cat, watching, 'then the

mouse will do me no harm if I eat it?'

'No,' said the Woman, braiding up her hair, 'eat it quickly and I will ever be grateful to you.'

Cat made one jump and caught the little mouse, and the Woman said, 'A hundred thanks. Even the First Friend is not quick enough to catch little mice as you have done. You must be very wise.'

That very moment and second, O Best Beloved, the Milk-pot that stood by the fire cracked in two piece – *ffft* – because it remembered the bargain she had made with the Cat; and when the Woman jumped down from the footstool – lo and behold! – the Cat was lapping up the warm white milk that lay in one of the broken pieces.

'O my Enemy and Wife of my Enemy and Mother of my Enemy,' said the Cat, 'it is I: for you have spoken three words in my praise, and now I can drink the warm white milk three times a day for always and always and always. But *still* I am the Cat who walks by himself, and all places are alike to me.'

Then the Woman laughed and set the Cat a bowl of the warm white milk and said, 'O Cat, you are as clever as a man, but remember that your bargain was not made with the Man or the Dog, and I do not know what they will do when they come home.'

'What is that to me?' said the Cat. 'If I

have my place in the Cave by the fire and my warm white milk three times a day I do not care what the Man or the Dog can do.'

That evening when the Man and the Dog came into the Cave, the Woman told them all the story of the bargain, while the Cat sat by the fire and smiled. Then the Man said, 'Yes, but he has not made a bargain with *me* or with all proper Men after me.' Then he took off his two leather boots and he took up his little stone axe (that makes three) and he fetched a piece of wood and a hatchet (that is five altogether), and he set them out in a row and he said, 'Now we will make *our* bargain. If you do not catch mice when you are in the Cave for always and always and always, I will throw these five things at you whenever I see you, and so shall all proper Men do after me.'

'Ah,' said the Woman, listening, 'this is a very clever Cat, but he is not so clever as my Man.'

The Cat counted the five things (and they looked very knobby) and he said, 'I will catch mice when I am in the Cave for always and always and always; but *still* I am the Cat who walks by himself, and all places are alike to me.'

'Not when I am near,' said the Man. 'If you had not said that last I would have put all these things away for always and always and always; but now I am going to throw my two boots and my little stone axe (that makes three) at you whenever I meet you. And so shall all proper Men do after me!'

Then the Dog said, 'Wait a minute. He has not made a bargain with *me* or with all proper Dogs after me.' And he showed his teeth and said, 'If you are not kind to the Baby while I am in the Cave for always and always and always, I will hunt you till I catch you, and when I catch you I will bite you. And so shall all proper Dogs do after me.'

'Ah,' said the Woman, listening, 'this is a very clever Cat, but he is not so clever as the Dog.'

Cat counted the Dog's teeth (and they looked very pointed) and he said, 'I will be kind to the Baby while I am in the Cave, as long as he does not pull my tail too hard, for always and always and always. But *still* I am the Cat that walks by himself, and all places are alike to me.'

'Not when I am near,' said the Dog. 'If you had not said that last I would have shut my mouth for always and always and always; but *now* I am going to hunt you up a tree whenever I meet you. And so shall all proper Dogs do after me.'

Then the Man threw his two boots and his little stone axe (that makes three) at the Cat, and the Cat ran out of the Cave and the Dog chased him up a tree; and from that day to this, Best Beloved, three proper Men out of five will always throw things at a Cat whenever they meet him, and all proper Dogs will chase him up a tree. But the Cat keeps his side of the bargain too. He will kill mice, and he will be kind to Babies when he is in the house, just as long as they do not pull his tail too hard. But when he has done that, and between times, and when the moon gets up and night comes, he is the Cat that walks by himself, and all places are alike to him. Then he goes out to the Wet Wild Woods or up the Wet Wild Trees or on the Wet Wild Roofs, waving his wild tail and walking by his wild lone.

PUSSY CAN SIT
BY THE FIRE
AND SING

Pussy can sit by the fire and sing,
Pussy can climb a tree,
Or play with a silly old cork and string
To 'muse herself, not me.
But I like *Binkie* my dog, because
He knows how to behave;
So, *Binkie's* the same as the First Friend
  was,
And I am the Man in the Cave!

Pussy will play Man Friday till
It's time to wet her paw
And make her walk on the window-sill
(For the footprint Crusoe saw);
Then she fluffles her tail and mews,
And scratches and won't attend.
But *Binkie* will play whatever I choose,
And he is my true First Friend!

Pussy will rub my knees with her head
Pretending she loves me hard;
But the very minute I go to my bed
Pussy runs out in the yard,
And there she stays till the morning-light;

So I know it is only pretend;
But *Binkie*, he snores at my feet all night,
And he is my Firstest Friend!

THE CONVERSION OF ST WILFRID

They had bought peppermints up at the village, and were coming home past little St Barnabas' church, when they saw Jimmy Kidbrooke, the carpenter's baby, kicking at the churchyard gate, with a shaving in his mouth and the tears running down his cheeks.

Una pulled out the shaving and put in a peppermint. Jimmy said he was looking for his grand-daddy – he never seemed to take much notice of his father – so they went up between the old graves, under the leaf-dropping limes, to the porch, where Jim trotted in, looked about the empty church, and screamed like a gate-hinge.

Young Sam Kidbrooke's voice came from the bell-tower, and made them jump.

'Why, Jimmy,' he called, 'what are you doin' here? Fetch him, Father!'

Old Mr Kidbrooke stumped downstairs, jerked Jimmy on to his shoulder, stared at the children beneath his brass spectacles, and stumped back again. They laughed: it was so exactly like Mr Kidbrooke.

'It's all right,' Una called up the stairs. 'We found him, Sam. Does his mother know?'

'He's come off by himself. She'll be just about crazy,' Sam answered.

'Then I'll run down street and tell her.' Una darted off.

'Thank you, Miss Una. Would you like to see how we're mendin' the bell-beams, Mus' Dan?'

Dan hopped up, and saw young Sam lying on his stomach in a most delightful place among beams and ropes, close to the five great bells. Old Mr Kidbrooke on the floor beneath was planing a piece of wood, and Jimmy was eating the shavings as fast as they came away. He never looked at Jimmy; Jimmy never stopped eating; and the broad gilt-bobbed pendulum of the church clock never stopped swinging across the white-washed wall of the tower.

Dan winked through the sawdust that fell on his up-turned face.

'Ring a bell,' he called.

'I mustn't do that, but I'll buzz one of 'em a bit for you,' said Sam. He pounded on the sound-bow of the biggest bell, and waked a hollow groaning boom that ran up and down the tower like creepy feelings down your back. Just when it almost began to hurt, it died away in a hurry of beautiful sorrowful cries, like a wine-glass rubbed with a wet finger. The pendulum clanked – one loud clank to each silent swing.

Dan heard Una return from Mrs

Kidbrooke's, and ran down to fetch her. She was standing by the font staring at someone who kneeled at the altar rail.

'Is that the Lady who practises the organ?' she whispered.

'No. She's gone into the organ-place. Besides, she wears black,' Dan replied.

The figure rose and came down the nave. It was a white-haired man in a long white gown with a sort of scarf looped low on the neck, one end hanging over his shoulder. His loose long sleeves were embroidered with gold, and a deep strip of gold embroidery waved and sparkled round the hem of his gown.

'Go and meet him,' said Puck's voice behind the font. 'It's only Wilfrid.'

'Wilfrid who?' said Dan. 'You come along too.'

'Wilfrid – Saint of Sussex, and Archbishop of York. *I* shall wait till he asks me.' He waved them forward. Their feet squeaked on the old grave slabs in the centre aisle. The Archbishop raised one hand with a pink ring on it, and said something in Latin. He was very handsome, and his thin face looked almost as silvery as his thin circle of hair.

'Are you alone?' he asked.

'Puck's here, of course,' said Una. 'Do you know him?'

'I know him better now than I used to.' He

beckoned over Dan's shoulder, and spoke again in Latin. Puck pattered forward, holding himself as straight as an arrow. The Archbishop smiled.

'Be welcome,' said he. 'Be very welcome.'

'Welcome to you also, O Prince of the Church,' Puck replied. The Archbishop bowed his head and passed on, till he glimmered like a white moth in the shadow by the font.

'He does look awfully princely,' said Una. 'Isn't he coming back?'

'Oh yes. He's only looking over the church. He's very fond of churches,' said Puck. 'What's that?'

The Lady who practises the organ was speaking to the blower-boy behind the organ-screen. 'We can't very well talk here,' Puck whispered. 'Let's go to Panama Corner.'

He led them to the end of the south aisle, where there is a slab of iron which says in queer, long-tailed letters: *Orate p. annema Jhone Coline.* The children always called it Panama Corner.

The Archbishop moved slowly about the little church, peering at the old memorial tablets and the new glass windows. The Lady who practises the organ began to pull out stops and rustle hymn-books behind the screen.

'I hope she'll do all the soft lacey tunes –

34

like treacle on porridge,' said Una.

'I like the trumpety ones best,' said Dan. 'Oh, look at Wilfrid! He's trying to shut the altar gates!'

'Tell him he mustn't,' said Puck, quite seriously.

'He can't, anyhow,' Dan muttered, and tip-toed out of Panama Corner while the Archbishop patted and patted at the carved gates that always sprang open again beneath his hand.

'That's no use, sir,' Dan whispered. 'Old Mr Kidbrooke says altar-gates are just *the* one pair of gates which no man can shut. He made 'em so himself.'

The Archbishop's blue eyes twinkled. Dan saw that he knew all about it.

'I beg your pardon,' Dan stammered – very angry with Puck.

'Yes, I know! He made them so Himself.' The Archbishop smiled, and crossed to Panama Corner, where Una dragged up a certain padded armchair for him to sit on.

The organ played softly. 'What does that music say?' he asked.

Una dropped into the chant without thinking: '"Oh, all ye works of the Lord, bless ye the Lord; praise him and magnify him for ever." We call it the Noah's Ark, because it's all lists of things – beasts and birds and whales, you know.'

'Whales?' said the Archbishop quickly.

'Yes – "O ye whales, and all that move in the waters,"' Una hummed – '"Bless ye the Lord" – it sounds like a wave turning over, doesn't it?'

'Holy Father,' said Puck with a demure face, 'is a little seal also "one who moves in the water"?'

'Eh? Oh yes – yess!' he laughed. 'A seal moves wonderfully in the waters. Do the seal come to my island still?'

Puck shook his head. 'All those little islands have been swept away.

'Very possible. The tides ran fiercely down there. Do you know the land of the Sea-calf, maiden?'

'No – but we've seen seals – at Brighton.'

'The Archbishop is thinking of a little farther down the coast. He means Seal's Eye – Selsea – down Chichester way – where he converted the South Saxons,' Puck explained.

'Yes – yess; if the South Saxons did not convert me,' said the Archbishop, smiling. 'The first time I was wrecked was on that coast. As our ship took ground and we tried to push her off, an old fat fellow, I remember, reared breast-high out of the water, and scratched his head with his flipper as if he were saying: 'What *does* that respectable person with the pole think he is doing?' I was very wet and miserable, but I could not help laughing, till the natives

36

came down and attacked us.'

'What did you do?' Dan asked.

'One couldn't very well go back to France, so one tried to make them go back to the shore. All the South Saxons are born wreckers, like my own Northumbrian folk. I was bringing over a few things for my old church at York, and some of the natives laid hands on them, and – and I'm afraid I lost my temper.'

'It is said,' Puck's voice was wickedly meek, 'that there was a great fight.'

'Eh, but I must ha' been a silly lad.'

Wilfrid spoke with a sudden thick burr in his voice. He coughed, and took up his silvery tones again. 'There was no fight really. My men thumped a few of them, but the tide rose half an hour before its time, with a strong wind, and we backed off. What I wanted to say, though, was, that the seas about us were full of sleek seals watching the scuffle. My good Eddi – my chaplain – insisted that they were demons. Yes – yess! That was my first acquaintance with the South Saxons and their seals.'

'But not the only time you were wrecked, was it?' said Dan.

'Alas, no! On sea and land my life seems to have been one long shipwreck.' He looked at the Jhone Coline slab as old Hobden sometimes looks into the fire. 'Ah, well!'

'But did you ever have any more adventures among the seals?' said Una, after a pause.

'Oh, the seals! I beg your pardon. They are the important things. Yes – yess! I went back to the South Saxons after twelve – fifteen – years. No, I did not come by water, but overland from my own Northumbria, to see what I could do. It's little one *can* do with that class of native except make them stop killing each other and themselves–'

'Why did they kill themselves?' Una asked, her chin in her hand.

'Because they were heathen. When they grew tired of life (as if they were the only people) they would jump into the sea. They called it going to Wotan. It wasn't want of food always – by any means. A man would tell you that he felt grey in the heart, or a woman would say that she saw nothing but long days in front of her; and they'd saunter away to the mud-flats and – that would be the end of them, poor souls, unless one headed them off! One had to run quick, but one can't allow people to lay hands on themselves because they happen to feel grey. Yes – yess! Extraordinary people, the South Saxons. Disheartening, sometimes... What does that say now?' The organ had changed tune again.

'Only a hymn for next Sunday,' said Una. '"The Church's One Foundation." Go on, please, about running over the mud. I

38

should like to have seen you.'

'I dare say you would, and I really *could* run in those days. Ethelwalch the king gave me some five or six muddy parishes by the sea, and the first time my good Eddi and I rode there we saw a man slouching along the slob, among the seals at Manhood End. My good Eddi disliked seals – but he swallowed his objections and ran like a hare.'

'Why?' said Dan.

'For the same reason that I did. We thought it was one of our people going to drown himself. As a matter of fact, Eddi and I were nearly drowned in the pools before we overtook him. To cut a long story short, we found ourselves very muddy, very breathless, being quietly made fun of in good Latin by a very well-spoken person. No – he'd no idea of going to Wotan. He was fishing on his own beaches, and he showed us the beacons and turf-heaps that divided his lands from the Church property. He took us to his own house, gave us a good dinner, some more than good wine, sent a guide with us into Chichester, and became one of my best and most refreshing friends. He was a Meon by descent, from the west edge of the kingdom; a scholar educated, curiously enough, at Lyons, my old school; had travelled the world over, even to Rome, and was a brilliant talker. We found we had scores of acquaintances in common. It seemed he was a small chief under King Ethelwalch, and I fancy the King was somewhat afraid of him. The South Saxons mistrust a man who talks too well. Ah! Now, I've left out the very point of my story. He kept a great grey-muzzled old dog-seal that he had brought up from a pup. He called it Padda – after one of my clergy. It *was* rather like fat, honest old Padda. The creature followed him everywhere, and nearly knocked down my good Eddi when we first met him. Eddi loathed it. It used to sniff at his thin legs and cough at him. I can't say I ever took much notice of it (I was not fond of animals), till one day Eddi came to me with a circumstantial account of some witchcraft that Meon worked. He would tell the seal to go down to the beach the last thing at night, and bring him word of the weather. When it came back, Meon might say to his slaves, "Padda thinks we shall have wind tomorrow. Haul up the boats." I spoke to Meon casually about the story, and he laughed.

'He told me he could judge by the look of the creature's coat and the way it sniffed what weather was brewing. Quite possible. One need not put down everything one does not understand to the work of bad spirits – or good ones, for that matter.' He nodded towards Puck, who nodded gaily in return.

'I say so,' he went on, 'because to a certain extent I have been made a victim of that habit of mind. Some while after I was settled at Selsea, King Ethelwalch and Queen Ebba ordered their people to be baptised. I fear I'm too old to believe that a whole nation can change its heart at the King's command, and I had a shrewd suspicion that their real motive was to get a good harvest. No rain had fallen for two or three years, but as soon as we had finished baptising, it fell heavily, and they all said it was a miracle.'

'And was it?' Dan asked.

'Everything in life is a miracle, but' – the Archbishop twisted the heavy ring on his finger – 'I should be slow – ve-ry slow should I be – to assume that a certain sort of miracle happens whenever lazy and improvident people say they are going to turn over a new leaf if they are paid for it. My friend Meon had sent his slaves to the font, but he had not come himself, so the next time I rode over – to return a manuscript – I took the liberty of asking why. He was perfectly open about it. He looked on the King's action as a heathen attempt to curry favour with the Christians' God through me the Archbishop, and he would have none of it. "My dear man," I said, "admitting that that is the case, surely you, as an educated person, don't believe in

Wotan and all the other hobgoblins any more than Padda here". The old seal was hunched up on his ox-hide behind his master's chair.

'"Even if I don't,' he said, 'why should I insult the memory of my fathers' gods? I have sent you a hundred and three of my rascals to christen. Isn't that enough?"

'"By no means," I answered. "I want *you*."

'"He wants us! What do you think of that, Padda?" He pulled the seal's whiskers till it threw back its head and roared, and he pretended to interpret. "No! Padda says he won't be baptised yet awhile. He says you'll stay to dinner and come fishing with me to-morrow, because you're overworked and need a rest."

'"I wish you'd keep yon brute in its proper place," I said, and Eddi, my chaplain, agreed.

'"I do,' said Meon. "I keep him just next my heart. He can't tell a lie, and he doesn't know how to love anyone except me. It 'ud be the same if I were dying on a mud-bank, wouldn't it, Padda?"

'"Augh! Augh!" said Padda, and put up his head to be scratched.

'Then Meon began to tease Eddi: "Padda says, if Eddi saw his Archbishop dying on a mud-bank Eddi would tuck up his gown and run. Padda knows Eddi can run too! Padda came into Wittering Church last Sunday – all wet – to hear the music, and Eddi ran out."

'My good Eddi rubbed his hands and his shins together, and flushed. "Padda is a child of the Devil, who is the father of lies!" he cried, and begged my pardon for having spoken. I forgave him.

'"Yes. You are just about stupid enough for a musician," said Meon. "But here he is. Sing a hymn to him and see if he can stand it. You'll find my small harp beside the fireplace."

'Eddi, who is really an excellent musician, played and sang for quite half an hour. Padda shuffled off his ox-hide, hunched himself on his flippers before him, and listened with his head thrown back. Yes – yess! A rather funny sight! Meon tried not to laugh, and asked Eddi if he were satisfied.

'It takes some time to get an idea out of my good Eddi's head. He looked at me.

'"Do you want to sprinkle him with holy water, and see if he flies up the chimney? Why not baptise him?" said Meon.

'Eddi was really shocked. I thought it was bad taste myself.

'"That's not fair," said Meon. "You call him a demon and a familiar spirit because he loves his master and likes music, and when I offer you a chance to prove it you won't take it. Look here! I'll make a bargain. I'll be baptised if you'll baptise Padda too.

He's more of a man than most of my slaves."

'"One doesn't bargain – or joke – about these matters," I said. He was going altogether too far.

'"Quite right," said Meon; "I shouldn't like any one to joke about Padda. Padda, go down to the beach and bring us tomorrow's weather."

'My good Eddi must have been a little overtired with his day's work. "I am a servant of the Church," he cried. "My business is to save souls, not to enter into fellowships and understandings with accursed beasts."

'"Have it your own narrow way," said Meon. "Padda, you needn't go." The old fellow flounced back to his ox-hide at once.

'"Man could learn obedience at least from that creature," said Eddi, a little ashamed of himself. Christians should not curse.

'"Don't begin to apologise just when I am beginning to like you," said Meon. "We'll leave Padda behind tomorrow – out of respect to your feelings. Now let's go to supper. We must be up early tomorrow for the whiting."

'The next was a beautiful crisp autumn morning – a weather breeder, if I had taken the trouble to think; but it's refreshing to escape from kings and converts for half a day. We three went by ourselves in Meon's smallest boat, and we got on the whiting near an old wreck, a mile or so off shore.

Meon knew the marks to a yard, and the fish were keen. Yes – yess! A perfect morning's fishing! If a bishop can't be a fisherman, who can?' He twiddled his ring again. 'We stayed there a little too long, and while we were getting up our stone, down came the fog. After some discussion, we decided to row for the land. The ebb was just beginning to make round the point, and sent us all ways at once like a coracle.'

'Selsea Bill,' said Puck under his breath. 'The tides run something furious there.'

'I believe you,' said the Archbishop. 'Meon and I have spent a good many evenings arguing as to where exactly we drifted. All I know is we found ourselves in a little rocky cove that had sprung up round us out of the fog, and a swell lifted the boat on to a ledge, and she broke up beneath our feet. We had just time to shuffle through the weed before the next wave. The sea was rising.

'"It's rather a pity we didn't let Padda go down to the beach last night," said Meon. "He might have warned us this was coming."

'"Better fall into the hands of God than the hands of demons," said Eddi, and his teeth chattered as he prayed. A nor'-west breeze had just got up – distinctly cool.

'"Save what you can of the boat," said Meon; "we may need it," and we had to

45

drench ourselves again, fishing out stray planks.'

'What for?' said Dan.

'For firewood. We did not know when we should get off. Eddi had flint and steel, and we found dry fuel in the old gulls' nests and lit a fire. It smoked abominably, and we guarded it with boat-planks up-ended between the rocks. One gets used to that sort of thing if one travels. Unluckily I'm not so strong as I was. I fear I must have been a trouble to my friends. It was blowing a full gale before midnight. Eddi wrung out his cloak, and tried to wrap me in it, but I ordered him on his obedience to keep it. However, he held me in his arms all the first night, and Meon begged his pardon for what he'd said the night before – about Eddi running away if he found me on a sandbank, you remember.

'"You are right in half your prophecy," said Eddi. "I have tucked up my gown, at any rate." (The wind had blown it over his head.) "Now let us thank God for His mercies."

'"Hum!" said Meon. "If this gale lasts, we stand a very fair chance of dying of starvation."

'"If it be God's will that we live, God will provide," said Eddi. "At least help me to sing to Him." The wind almost whipped the words out of his mouth, but he braced himself against a rock and sang psalms.

'I'm glad I never concealed my opinion – from myself – that Eddi was a better man than I. Yet I have worked hard in my time – very hard! Yes – yess! So the morning and the evening were our second day on that islet. There was rain-water in the rock pools, and, as a Churchman, I knew how to fast, but I admit we were hungry. Meon fed our fire chip by chip to eke it out, and they made me sit over it, the dear fellows, when I was too weak to object. Meon held me in his arms the second night, just like a child. My good Eddi was a little out of his senses, and imagined himself teaching a York choir to sing. Even so, he was beautifully patient with them.

'I heard Meon whisper, "If this keeps up we shall go to our gods. I wonder what Wotan will say to me. He must know I don't believe in him. On the other hand, I can't do what Ethelwalch finds so easy – curry favour with your God at the last minute, in the hope of being saved – as you call it. How do you advise, Bishop?"

'"My dear man," I said, "if that is your honest belief, I take it upon myself to say you had far better not curry favour with any god. But if it's only your Jutish pride that holds you back, lift me up, and I'll baptise you even now."

'"Lie still," said Meon. "I could judge

better if I were in my own hall. But to desert one's fathers' gods – even if one doesn't believe in them – in the middle of a gale, isn't quite– What would you do yourself?"

'I was lying in his arms, kept alive by the warmth of his big, steady heart. It did not seem to me the time or the place for subtle arguments, so I answered, "No, I certainly should not desert my God." I don't see even now what else I could have said.

'"Thank you. I'll remember that, if I live," said Meon, and I must have drifted back to my dreams about Northumbria and beautiful France, for it was broad daylight when I heard him calling on Wotan in that high, shaking heathen yell that I detest so.

'"Lie quiet. I'm giving Wotan his chance," he said. Our dear Eddi ambled up, still beating time to his imaginary choir.

'"Yes. Call on your gods," he cried, "and see what gifts they will send you. They are gone on a journey, or they are hunting."

'I assure you the words were not out of his mouth when old Padda shot from the top of a cold wrinkled swell, drove himself over the weedy ledge, and landed fair in our laps with a rock-cod between his teeth. I could not help smiling at Eddi's face. "A miracle! A miracle!" he cried, and kneeled down to clean the cod.

'"You've been a long time finding us, my

son," said Meon. "Now fish – fish for all our lives. We're starving, Padda."

'The old fellow flung himself quivering like a salmon backward into the boil of the currents round the rocks, and Meon said, "We're safe. I'll send him to fetch help when this wind drops. Eat and be thankful."

'I never tasted anything so good as those rock-codlings we took from Padda's mouth and half roasted over the fire. Between his plunges Padda would hunch up and purr over Meon with the tears running down his face. I never knew before that seals could weep for joy – as I have wept.

'"Surely," said Eddi, with his mouth full, "God has made the seal the loveliest of His creatures in the water. Look how Padda breasts the current! He stands up against it like a rock; now watch the chain of bubbles where he dives; and now – there is his wise head under that rock ledge! Oh, a blessing be on thee, my little brother Padda!"

'"You *said* he was a child of the Devil!" Meon laughed.

'"There I sinned," poor Eddi answered. "Call him here, and I will ask his pardon. God sent him out of the storm to humble me, a fool."

'"I won't ask you to enter into fellowships and understandings with any accursed brute," said Meon, rather unkindly. "Shall we say he was sent to our Bishop as the ravens were sent to your prophet Elijah?"

'"Doubtless that is so," said Eddi. "I will write it so if I live to get home."

'"No – no!" I said. "Let us three poor men kneel and thank God for His mercies."

'We kneeled, and old Padda shuffled up and thrust his head under Meon's elbows. I laid my hand upon it and blessed him. So did Eddi.

'"And now, my son," I said to Meon, "shall I baptise thee?"

'"Not yet," said he. "Wait till we are well ashore and at home. No God in any Heaven shall say that I came to him or left him because I was wet and cold. I will send Padda to my people for a boat. Is that witchcraft, Eddi?"

'"Why, no. Surely Padda will go and pull them to the beach by the skirts of their gowns as he pulled me in Wittering Church to ask me to sing. Only then I was afraid, and did not understand," said Eddi.

'"You are understanding now," said Meon, and at a wave of his arm off went Padda to the mainland, making a wake like a war-boat till we lost him in the rain. Meon's people could not bring a boat across for some hours; even so it was ticklish work among the rocks in that tideway. But they hoisted me aboard, too stiff to move, and Padda swam behind us, barking and turning somersaults all the way to Manhood End!'

50

'Good old Padda!' murmured Dan.

'When we were quite rested and re-clothed, and his people had been summoned – not an hour before – Meon offered himself to be baptised.'

'Was Padda baptised too?' Una asked.

'No, that was only Meon's joke. But he sat blinking on his ox-hide in the middle of the hall. When Eddi (who thought I wasn't looking) made a little cross in holy water on his wet muzzle, he kissed Eddi's hand. A week before Eddi wouldn't have touched him. *That* was a miracle, if you like! But seriously, I was more glad than I can tell you to get Meon. A rare and splendid soul that never looked back – never looked back!' The Archbishop half closed his eyes.

'But, sir,' said Puck, most respectfully, 'haven't you left out what Meon said after-wards?' Before the Archbishop could speak he turned to the children and went on: 'Meon called all his fishers and ploughmen and herdsmen into the hall and he said: "Listen, men! Two days ago I asked our Bishop whether it was fair for a man to desert his fathers' gods in a time of danger. Our Bishop said it was not fair. You needn't shout like that, because you are all Chris-tians now. My red war-boat's crew will remember how near we all were to death when Padda fetched them over to the Bishop's islet. You can tell your mates that

51

even in that place, at that time, hanging on the wet, weedy edge of death, our Bishop, a Christian, counselled me, a heathen, to stand by my fathers' gods. I tell you now that a faith which takes care that every man shall keep faith, even though he may save his soul by breaking faith, is the faith for a man to believe in. So I believe in the Christian God, and in Wilfrid His Archbishop, and in the Church that Wilfrid rules. You have been baptised once by the King's orders. I shall not have you baptised again; but if I find any more old women being sent to Wotan, or any girls dancing on the sly before Balder, or any men talking about Thun or Lok or the rest, I will teach you with my own hands how to keep faith with the Christian God. Go out quietly; you'll find a couple of beefs on the beach.' Then of course they shouted 'Hurrah!' which meant 'Thor help us!' and – I think you laughed, sir?'

'I think you remember it all too well,' said the Archbishop, smiling. 'It was a joyful day for me. I had learned a great deal on that rock where Padda found us. Yes – yess! One should deal kindly with all the creatures of God, and gently with their masters. But one learns late.'

He rose, and his gold-embroidered sleeves rustled thickly.

The organ clacked and took deep breaths.

'Wait a minute,' Dan whispered. 'She's

going to do the trumpety one. It takes all the wind you can pump. It's in Latin, sir.'

'There is no other tongue,' the Archbishop answered.

'It's not a real hymn,' Una explained. 'She does it as a treat after her exercises. She isn't a real organist, you know. She just comes down here sometimes, from the Albert Hall.'

'Oh, what a miracle of a voice!' said the Archbishop.

It rang out suddenly from a dark arch of lonely noises – every word spoken to the very end.

'Dies Irae, dies illa
Solvet saeclum in favilla
Teste David cum Sibylla.'

The Archbishop caught his breath and moved forward.

The music carried on by itself a while.

'Now it's calling all the light out of the windows,' Una whispered to Dan.

'I think it's more like a horse neighing in battle,' he whispered back. The voice cried:

'Tuba mirum spargens sonum
Per sepulchra regionum.'

Deeper and deeper the organ dived down, but far below its deepest note they heard Puck's voice joining in the last line:

'Coget omnes ante thronum.'

As they looked in wonder, for it sounded like the dull jar of one of the very pillars shifting, the little fellow turned and went out through the south door.

'Now's the sorrowful part, but it's very beautiful.' Una found herself speaking to the empty chair in front of her.

'What are you doing that for?' Dan said behind her. 'You spoke so politely too.'

'I don't know... I thought...' said Una. 'Funny!'

''Tisn't. It's the part you like best,' Dan grunted.

The music had turned soft – full of little sounds that chased each other on wings across the broad gentle flood of the main tune. But the voice was ten times lovelier than the music.

'Recordare Jesu pie,
Quod sum causa
Tuae viae,
Ne me perdas illâ die!'

There was no more. They moved out into the centre-aisle.

'That you?' the Lady called as she shut the lid. 'I thought I heard you, and I played it on purpose.'

'Thank you awfully,' said Dan. 'We hoped you would, so we waited. Come on, Una, it's pretty nearly dinner-time.'

GARM – A HOSTAGE

One night, a very long time ago, I drove to an Indian military cantonment called Mian Mir to see amateur theatricals. At the back of the Infantry barracks a soldier, his cap over one eye, rushed in front of the horses and shouted that he was a dangerous highway robber. As a matter of fact he was a friend of mine, so I told him to go home before anyone caught him; but he fell under the pole, and I heard voices of a military guard in search of someone.

The driver and I coaxed him into the carriage, drove home swiftly, undressed him and put him to bed, where he waked next morning with a sore headache, very much ashamed. When his uniform was cleaned and dried, and he had been shaved and washed and made neat, I drove him back to barracks with his arm in a fine white sling, and reported that I had accidentally run over him. I did not tell this story to my friend's sergeant, who was a hostile and unbelieving person, but to his lieutenant, who did not know us quite so well.

Three days later my friend came to call, and at his heels slobbered and fawned one of the finest bull-terriers – of the old-fashioned breed, two parts bull and one terrier – that I had ever set eyes on. He was pure white, with a fawn-coloured saddle just behind his neck, and a fawn diamond at the root of his thin whippy tail. I had admired him distantly for more than a year; and Vixen, my own fox-terrier, knew him too, but did not approve.

''E's for you,' said my friend; but he did not look as though he liked parting with him.

'Nonsense! That dog's worth more than most men, Stanley,' I said.

''E's that and more. 'Tention!'

The dog rose on his hind legs, and stood upright for a full minute.

'Eyes right!'

He sat on his haunches and turned his head sharp to the right. At a sign he rose and barked thrice. Then he shook hands with his right paw and bounded lightly to my shoulder. Here he made himself into a necktie, limp and lifeless, hanging down on either side of my neck. I was told to pick him up and throw him in the air. He fell with a howl, and held up one leg.

'Part o' the trick,' said his owner. 'You're going to die now. Dig yourself your little grave an' shut your little eye.'

Still limping, the dog hobbled to the garden-edge, dug a hole and lay down in it.

When told that he was cured he jumped out, wagging his tail, and whining for applause. He was put through half a dozen other tricks, such as showing how he would hold a man safe (I was that man, and he sat down before me, his teeth bared, ready to spring), and how he would stop eating at the word of command. I had no more than finished praising him when my friend made a gesture that stopped the dog as though he had been shot, took a piece of blue-ruled canteen-paper from his helmet, handed it to me and ran away, while the dog looked after him and howled. I read

SIR – I give you the dog because of what you got me out of. He is the best I know, for I made him myself, and he is as good as a man. Please do not give him too much to eat, and please do not give him back to me, for I'm not going to take him, if you will keep him. So please do not try to give him back any more. I have kept his name back, so you can call him anything and he will answer, but please do not give him back. He can kill a man as easy as anything, but please do not give him too much meat. He knows more than a man.

Vixen sympathetically joined her shrill little yap to the bull-terrier's despairing cry, and I was annoyed, for I knew that a man who

58

cares for dogs is one thing, but a man who loves one dog is quite another. Dogs are at the best no more than verminous vagrants, self-scratchers, foul feeders, and unclean by the law of Moses and Mohammed; but a dog with whom one lives alone for at least six months in the year; a free thing, tied to you so strictly by love that without you he will not stir or exercise; a patient, temperate, humorous, wise soul, who knows your moods before you know them yourself, is not a dog under any ruling.

I had Vixen, who was all my dog to me; and I felt what my friend must have felt, at tearing out his heart in this style and leaving it in my garden. However, the dog understood clearly enough that I was his master, and did not follow the soldier. As soon as he drew breath I made much of him, and Vixen, yelling with jealousy, flew at him. Had she been of his own sex, he might have cheered himself with a fight, but he only looked worriedly when she nipped his deep iron sides, laid his heavy head on my knee, and howled anew. I meant to dine at the Club that night, but as darkness drew in, and the dog snuffed through the empty house like a child trying to recover from a fit of sobbing, I felt that I could not leave him to suffer his first evening alone. So we fed at home, Vixen on one side and the stranger-dog on the other; she watching his every mouthful, and saying explicitly what she thought of his table manners, which were much better than hers.

It was Vixen's custom, till the weather grew hot, to sleep in my bed, her head on the pillow like a Christian; and when morning came I would always find that the little thing had braced her feet against the wall and pushed me to the very edge of the cot. This night she hurried to bed purposefully, every hair up, one eye on the stranger, who had dropped on a mat in a helpless, hopeless sort of way, all four feet spread out, sighing heavily. She settled her head on the pillow several times, to show her little airs and graces, and struck up her usual whiney sing-song before slumber. The stranger-dog softly edged towards me. I put out my hand and he licked it. Instantly my wrist was between Vixen's teeth, and her warning *aaarh!* said as plainly as speech, that if I took any further notice of the stranger she would bite.

I caught her behind her fat neck with my left hand, shook her severely, and said:

'Vixen, if you do that again you'll be put into the veranda. Now, remember!'

She understood perfectly, but the minute I released her she mouthed my right wrist once more, and waited with her ears back and all her body flattened, ready to bite. The big dog's tail thumped the floor in a humble and peace-making way.

I grabbed Vixen a second time, lifted her out of bed like a rabbit (she hated that and yelled), and, as I had promised, set her out in the veranda with the bats and the moonlight. At this she howled. Then she used coarse language – not to me, but to the bull-terrier – till she coughed with exhaustion. Then she ran round the house trying every door. Then she went off to the stables and barked as though someone were stealing the horses, which was an old trick of hers. Last she returned, and her snuffing yelp said, 'I'll be good! Let me in and I'll be good!'

She was admitted and flew to her pillow. When she was quieted I whispered to the other dog, 'You can lie on the foot of the bed.' The bull jumped up at once, and though I felt Vixen quiver with rage, she knew better than to protest. So we slept till the morning, and they had early breakfast with me, bite for bite, till the horse came round and we went for a ride. I don't think the bull had ever followed a horse before. He was wild with excitement, and Vixen, as usual, squealed and scuttered and scooted, and took charge of the procession.

There was one corner of a village near by, which we generally passed with caution, because all the yellow pariah-dogs of the place gathered about it. They were half-wild, starving beasts, and though utter cowards, yet where nine or ten of them get together they will mob and kill and eat an English dog. I kept a whip with a long lash for them. That morning they attacked Vixen, who, perhaps of design, had moved from beyond my horse's shadow.

The bull was ploughing along in the dust, fifty yards behind, rolling in his run, and smiling as bull-terriers will. I heard Vixen squeal; half a dozen of the curs closed in on her; a white streak came up behind me; a cloud of dust rose near Vixen, and, when it cleared, I saw one tall pariah with his back broken, and the bull wrenching another to earth. Vixen retreated to the protection of my whip, and the bull paddled back smiling more than ever, covered with the blood of his enemies. That decided me to call him 'Garm of the Bloody Breast,' who was a great person in his time, or 'Garm' for short; so, leaning forward, I told him what his temporary name would be. He looked up while I repeated it, and then raced away. I shouted 'Garm!' He stopped, raced back, and came up to ask my will.

Then I saw that my soldier friend was right, and that that dog knew and was worth more than a man. At the end of the ride I gave an order which Vixen knew and hated: 'Go away and get washed!' I said. Garm understood some part of it, and Vixen interpreted the rest, and the two trotted off together soberly. When I went to the back veranda Vixen had been washed snowy-white, and was very proud of herself, but the dog-boy would not touch Garm on any account unless I stood by. So I waited while he was being scrubbed, and Garm, with the soap creaming on the top of his broad head, looked at me to make sure that this was what I expected him to endure. He knew perfectly that the dog-boy was only obeying orders.

'Another time,' I said to the dog-boy, 'you will wash the great dog with Vixen when I send them home.'

'Does *he* know?' said the dog-boy, who understood the ways of dogs.

'Garm,' I said, 'another time you will be washed with Vixen.'

I knew that Garm understood. Indeed, next washing-day, when Vixen as usual fled under my bed, Garm stared at the doubtful dog-boy in the veranda, stalked to the place where he had been washed last time, and stood rigid in the tub.

But the long days in my office tried him sorely. We three would drive off in the morning at half-past eight and come home at six or later. Vixen, knowing the routine of it, went to sleep under my table; but the confinement ate into Garm's soul. He gener-ally sat on the veranda looking out on the

Mall; and well I knew what he expected.

Sometimes a company of soldiers would move along on their way to the Fort, and Garm rolled forth to inspect them; or an officer in uniform entered into the office, and it was pitiful to see poor Garm's welcome to the cloth – not the man. He would leap at him, and sniff and bark joyously, then run to the door and back again. One afternoon I heard him bay with a full throat – a thing I had never heard before – and he disappeared. When I drove into my garden at the end of the day a soldier in white uniform scrambled over the wall at the far end, and the Garm that met me was a joyous dog. This happened twice or thrice a week for a month.

I pretended not to notice, but Garm knew and Vixen knew. He would glide homewards from the office about four o'clock, as though he were only going to look at the scenery, and this he did so quietly that but for Vixen I should not have noticed him. The jealous little dog under the table would give a sniff and a snort, just loud enough to call my attention to the flight. Garm might go out forty times in the day and Vixen would never stir, but when he slunk off to see his true master in my garden she told me in her own tongue. That was the one sign she made to prove that Garm did not altogether belong to the family. They were the best of friends at all times, *but*, Vixen explained that I was not to forget Garm did not love me as she loved me.

I never expected it. The dog was not my dog – could never be my dog – and I knew he was as miserable as his master who tramped eight miles a day to see him. So it seemed to me that the sooner the two were reunited the better for all. One afternoon I sent Vixen home alone in the dogcart (Garm had gone before), and rode over to cantonments to find another friend of mine, who was an Irish soldier and a great friend of the dog's master.

I explained the whole case, and wound up with:

'And now Stanley's in my garden crying over his dog. Why doesn't he take him back? They're both unhappy.'

'Unhappy! There's no sense in the little man any more. But 'tis his fit.'

'What is his fit? He travels fifty miles a week to see the brute, and he pretends not to notice me when he sees me on the road; and I'm as unhappy as he is. Make him take the dog back.'

'It's his penance he's set himself. I told him by way of a joke, after you'd run over him so convenient that night, whin he was drunk – I said if he was a Catholic he'd do penance. Off he went wid that fit in his little head *an'* a dose of fever, an' nothing would

65

suit but givin' you the dog as a hostage.'

'Hostage for what? I don't want hostages from Stanley.'

'For his good behaviour. He's keepin' straight now, the way it's no pleasure to associate wid him.'

'Has he taken the pledge?'

'If 'twas only that I need not care. Ye can take the pledge for three months on an' off. He sez he'll never see the dog again, an' so, mark you, he'll keep straight for evermore. Ye know his fits? Well, this is wan of them. How's the dog takin' it?'

'Like a man. He's the best dog in India. Can't you make Stanley take him back?'

'I can do no more than I have done. But ye know his fits. He's just doin' his penance.'

'What will he do when he goes to the Hills? The doctor's put him on the list.'

It is the custom in India to send a certain number of invalids from each regiment up to stations in the Himalayas for the hot weather; and though the men ought to enjoy the cool and the comfort, they miss the society of the barracks down below, and do their best to come back or to avoid going. I felt that this move would bring matters to a head, so I left Terence hopefully, though he called after me – 'He won't take the dog, sorr. You can lay your month's pay on that. Ye know his fits.'

I never pretended to understand Private

Ortheris; and so I did the next best thing –
I left him alone.

That summer the invalids of the regiment
to which my friend belonged were ordered
off to the Hills early, because the doctors
thought marching in the cool of the day
would do them good. Their route lay south
to a place called Umballa, a hundred and
twenty miles or more. Then they would
turn east and march up into the hills to
Kasauli or Dugshai or Subathoo. I dined
with the officers the night before they left –
they were marching at five in the morning.
It was midnight when I drove into my
garden and surprised a white figure flying
over the wall.

'That man,' said my butler, 'has been here
since nine, making talk to that dog. He is
quite mad. I did not tell him to go away,
because he has been here many times
before, and because the dog-boy told me
that if I told him to go away, that great dog
would immediately slay me. He did not wish
to speak to the Protector of the Poor, and he
did not ask for anything to eat or drink.'

'Kadir Buksh,' said I, 'that was well done,
for the dog would surely have killed thee.
But I do not think the white soldier will
come any more.'

Garm slept ill that night and whimpered
in his dreams. Once he sprang up with a
clear, ringing bark, and I heard him wag his

tail till it waked him and the bark died out in a howl. He had dreamed he was with his master again, and I nearly cried. It was all Stanley's silly fault.

The first halt which the detachment of invalids made was some miles from their barracks, on the Amritsar road, and ten miles distant from my house. By a mere chance one of the officers drove back for another good dinner at the Club (cooking on the line of march is always bad), and there I met him. He was a particular friend of mine, and I knew that he knew how to love a dog properly. His pet was a big fat retriever who was going up to the Hills for his health, and, though it was still April, the round, brown brute puffed and panted in the Club veranda as though he would burst.

'It's amazing,' said the officer, 'what excuses these invalids of mine make to get back to barracks. There's a man in my company now asked me for leave to go back to cantonments to pay a debt he'd forgotten. I was so taken by the idea I let him go, and he jingled off in an *ekka* as pleased as Punch. Ten miles to pay a debt! Wonder what it was really?'

'If you'll drive me home I think I can show you,' I said.

So we went over to my house in his dog-cart with the retriever; and on the way I told him the story of Garm.

'I was wondering where that brute had gone to. He's the best dog in the regiment,' said my friend. 'I offered the little fellow twenty rupees for him a month ago. But he's a hostage, you say, for Stanley's good conduct. Stanley's one of the best men I have – when he chooses.'

'That's the reason why,' I said. 'A second-rate man wouldn't have taken things to heart as he has done.'

We drove in quietly at the far end of the garden, and crept round the house. There was a place close to the wall all grown about with tamarisk trees, where I knew Garm kept his bones. Even Vixen was not allowed to sit near it. In the full Indian moonlight I could see a white uniform bending over the dog.

'Goodbye, old man,' we could not help hearing Stanley's voice. 'For 'Eving's sake don't get bit and go mad by any measly pi-dog. But you can look after yourself, old man. *You* don't get drunk an' run about 'ittin' your friends. You takes your bones an' you eats your biscuit, an' you kills your enemy like a gentleman. I'm goin' away – don't 'owl – I'm goin' off to Kasauli, where I won't see you no more.'

I could hear him holding Garm's nose as the dog threw it up to the stars.

'You'll stay here an' be'ave, an' – an' I'll go

away an try to be'ave, an' I don't know 'ow to leave you. I don't know–'

'I think this is damn' silly,' said the officer, patting his foolish fubsy old retriever. He called to the private, who leaped to his feet, marched forward, and saluted.

'You here?' said the officer, turning away his head.

'Yes, sir, but I'm just goin' back.'

'I shall be leaving here at eleven in my cart. You come with me, I can't have sick men running about all over the place. Report yourself at eleven, *here*.'

We did not say much when we went indoors, but the officer muttered and pulled his retriever's ears.

He was a disgraceful, overfed doormat of a dog; and when he waddled off to my cookhouse to be fed, I had a brilliant idea.

At eleven o'clock that officer's dog was nowhere to be found, and you never heard such a fuss as his owner made. He called and shouted and grew angry, and hunted through my garden for half an hour.

Then I said: 'He's sure to turn up in the morning. Send a man in by rail, and I'll find the beast and return him.'

'Beast?' said the officer. 'I value that dog considerably more than I value any man I know. It's all very fine for you to talk – your dog's here.'

So she was – under my feet – and, had she

been missing, food and wages would have stopped in my house till her return. But some people grow fond of dogs not worth a cut of the whip. My friend had to drive away at last with Stanley in the back-seat and then the dog-boy said to me:

'What kind of animal is Bullen Sahib's dog? Look at him!'

I went to the boy's hut, and the fat old reprobate was lying on a mat carefully chained up. He must have heard his master calling for twenty minutes, but had not even attempted to join him.

'He has no face,' said the dog-boy scornfully. 'He is a *punniarkooter* (a spaniel). He never tried to get that cloth off his jaws when his master called. Now Vixen-baba would have jumped through the window, and that Great Dog would have slain me with his muzzled mouth. It is true that there are many kinds of dogs.'

Next evening who should turn up but Stanley. The officer had sent him back fourteen miles by rail with a note begging me to return the retriever if I had found him, and, if I had not, to offer huge rewards. The last train to camp left at half-past ten, and Stanley stayed till ten talking to Garm. I argued and entreated, and even threatened to shoot the bull-terrier, but the little man was as firm as a rock, though I gave him a good dinner and talked to him most severely. Garm knew as well as I that this was the last time he could hope to see his man, and followed Stanley like a shadow. The retriever said nothing, but licked his lips after his meal and waddled off without so much as saying 'Thank you' to the disgusted dog-boy.

So that last meeting was over and I felt as wretched as Garm, who moaned in his sleep all night. When we went to the office he found a place under the table close to Vixen, and dropped flat till it was time to go home. There was no more running out into the verandas, no slinking away for stolen talks with Stanley. As the weather grew warmer the dogs were forbidden to run beside the cart, but sat at my side on the seat, Vixen with her head under the crook of my left elbow, and Garm hugging the left handrail.

Here Vixen was ever in great form. She had to attend to all the moving traffic, such as bullock-carts that blocked the way, and camels, and led ponies; as well as to keep up her dignity when she passed low friends running in the dust. She never yapped for yapping's sake, but her shrill, high bark was known all along the Mall, and other men's terriers ki-yied in reply, and bullock-drivers looked over their shoulders and gave us the road with a grin.

But Garm cared for none of these things.

His big eyes were on the horizon and his terrible mouth was shut. There was another dog in the office who belonged to my chief. We called him 'Bob the Librarian,' because he always imagined vain rats behind the bookshelves, and in hunting for them would drag out half the old newspaper-files. Bob was a well-meaning idiot, but Garm did not encourage him. He would slide his head round the door, panting, 'Rats! Come along, Garm!' and Garm would shift one fore-paw over the other, and curl himself round, leaving Bob to whine at a most uninterested back. The office was nearly as cheerful as a tomb in those days.

Once, and only once, did I see Garm at all contented with his surroundings. He had gone for an unauthorised walk with Vixen early one Sunday morning, and a very young and foolish artillery-man (his battery had just moved to that part of the world) tried to steal them both. Vixen, of course, knew better than to take food from soldiers, and, besides, she had just finished her breakfast. So she trotted back with a large piece of the mutton that they issue to our troops, laid it down on my veranda, and looked up to see what I thought. I asked her where Garm was, and she ran in front of the horse to show me the way.

About a mile up the road we came across our artilleryman sitting very stiffly on the edge of a culvert with a greasy handkerchief on his knees. Garm was in front of him, looking rather pleased. When the man moved leg or hand, Garm bared his teeth in silence. A broken string hung from his collar, and the other half of it lay, all warm, in the artilleryman's still hand. He explained to me, keeping his eyes straight in front of him, that he had met this dog (he called him awful names) walking alone, and was going to take him to the Fort to be killed for a masterless pariah.

I said that Garm did not seem to me much of a pariah, but that he had better take him to the Fort if he thought best. He said he did not care to do so. I told him to go to the Fort alone. He said he did not want to go at that hour, but would follow my advice as soon as I had called off the dog. I instructed Garm to take him to the Fort, and Garm marched him solemnly up to the gate, one mile and a half under a hot sun, and I told the quarter-guard what had happened; but the young artilleryman was more angry than was at all necessary when they began to laugh. Several regiments, he was told, had tried to steal Garm in their time.

That month the hot weather shut down in earnest, and the dogs slept in the bathroom on the cool wet bricks where the bath is placed. Every morning, as soon as the man filled my bath, the two jumped in, and every morning the man filled the bath a second time. I said to him that he might as well fill a small tub specially for the dogs. 'Nay,' said he smiling, 'it is not their custom. They would not understand. Besides, the big bath gives them more space.'

The punkah-coolies who pull the punkahs day and night came to know Garm intimately. He noticed that when the swaying fan stopped I would call out to the coolie and bid him pull with a long stroke. If the man still slept I would wake him up. He discovered, too, that it was a good thing to lie in the wave of air under the punkah. Maybe Stanley had taught him all about this in barracks. At any rate, when the punkah stopped, Garm would first growl and cock his eye at the rope, and if that did not wake the man – it nearly always did – he would tiptoe forth and talk in the sleeper's ear. Vixen was a clever little dog, but she could never connect the punkah and the coolie; so Garm gave me grateful hours of cool sleep. But he was utterly wretched – as miserable as a human being; and in his misery he clung so closely to me that other men noticed it, and were envious. If I moved from one room to another Garm followed; if my pen stopped scratching, Garm's head was thrust into my hand; if I turned, half awake, on the pillow, Garm was up and at my side, for he knew that I was his only link with his master, and day and night, and night and day, his eyes asked one question – 'When is this going to end?'

Living with the dog as I did, I never noticed that he was more than ordinarily upset by the hot weather, till one day at the Club a man said: 'That dog of yours will die in a week or two. He's a shadow.' Then I dosed Garm with iron and quinine, which he hated; and I felt very anxious. He lost his appetite, and Vixen was allowed to eat his dinner under his eyes. Even that did not make him swallow, and we held a consultation on him, of the best man-doctor in the place; a lady-doctor, who cured the sick wives of kings; and the Deputy Inspector-General of the veterinary service of all India. They pronounced upon his symptoms, and I told them his story, and Garm lay on a sofa licking my hand.

'He's dying of a broken heart,' said the lady-doctor suddenly.

''Pon my word,' said the Deputy Inspector-General, 'I believe Mrs Macrae is perfectly right – as usual.'

The best man-doctor in the place wrote a prescription, and the veterinary Deputy Inspector-General went over it afterwards to be sure that the drugs were in the proper dog-proportions; and that was the first time in his life that our doctor ever allowed his prescriptions to be edited. It was a strong tonic, and it put the dear boy on his feet for a week or two; then he lost flesh again. I asked a man I knew to take him up to the Hills with him when he went, and the man came to the door with his kit packed on the top of the carriage. Garm took in the situation at one red glance. The hair rose along his back; he sat down in front of me and delivered the most awful growl I have ever heard in the jaws of a dog. I shouted to my friend to get away at once, and as soon as the carriage was out of the garden Garm laid his head on my knee and whined. So I knew his answer, and devoted myself to getting Stanley's address in the Hills.

My turn to go to the cool came late in August. We were allowed thirty days' holiday in a year, if no one fell sick, and we took it as we could be spared. My chief and Bob the Librarian had their holiday first, and when they were gone I made a calendar, as I always did, and hung it up at the head of my cot, tearing off one day at a time till they returned. Vixen had gone up to the Hills with me five times before; and she appreciated the cold and the damp and the beautiful wood fires there as much as I did.

'Garm,' I said, 'we are going back to Stanley at Kasauli. Kasauli – Stanley; Stanley – Kasauli.' And I repeated it twenty times. It was not Kasauli really, but another place. Still I remembered what Stanley had said in my garden on the last night, and I dared not change the name. Then Garm began to tremble; then he barked; and then he leaped up at me, frisking and wagging his tail.

'Not now,' I said, holding up my hand. 'When I say "Go," we'll go, Garm.' I pulled out the little blanket coat and spiked collar that Vixen always wore up in the Hills, to protect her against sudden chills and thieving leopards, and I let the two smell them and talk it over. What they said of course I do not know, but it made a new dog of Garm. His eyes were bright; and he barked joyfully when I spoke to him. He ate his food, and he killed his rats for the next three weeks, and when he began to whine I had only to say 'Stanley – Kasauli; Kasauli – Stanley,' to wake him up. I wish I had thought of it before.

My chief came back, all brown with living in the open air, and very angry at finding it so hot in the Plains. That same afternoon we three and Kadir Buksh began to pack for our month's holiday, Vixen rolling in and out of the bullock-trunk twenty times a minute, and Garm grinning all over and thumping on the floor with his tail. Vixen knew the routine of travelling as well as she knew my office-work. She went to the station, singing songs, on the front seat of the carriage, while Garm sat with me. She hurried into the railway carriage, saw Kadir

Buksh make up my bed for the night, got her drink of water, and curled up with her black-patch eye on the tumult of the platform. Garm followed her (the crowd gave him a lane all to himself) and sat down on the pillow with his eyes blazing, and his tail a haze behind him.

We came to Umballa in the hot misty dawn, four or five men, who had been working hard for eleven months, shouting for our dâks – the two-horse travelling carriages that were to take us up to Kalka at the foot of the Hills. It was all new to Garm. He did not understand carriages where you lay at full length on your bedding, but Vixen knew and hopped into her place at once; Garm following. The Kalka Road, before the railway was built, was about forty-seven miles long, and the horses were changed every eight miles. Most of them jibbed, and kicked, and plunged, but they had to go, and they went rather better than usual for Garm's deep bay in their rear.

There was a river to be forded, and four bullocks pulled the carriage, and Vixen stuck her head out of the sliding-door and nearly fell into the water while she gave directions. Garm was silent and curious, and rather needed reassuring about Stanley and Kasauli. So we rolled, barking and yelping, into Kalka for lunch, and Garm ate enough for two.

After Kalka the road wound among the hills, and we took a curricle with half-broken ponies, which were changed every six miles. No one dreamed of a railroad to Simla in those days, for it was seven thousand feet up in the air. The road was more than fifty miles long, and the regulation pace was just as fast as the ponies could go. Here, again, Vixen led Garm from one carriage to the other; jumped into the back seat, and shouted. A cool breath from the snows met us about five miles out of Kalka, and she whined for her coat, wisely fearing a chill on the liver. I had had one made for Garm too, and, as we climbed to the fresh breezes, I put it on, and Garm chewed it uncomprehendingly, but I think he was grateful.

'Hi-yi-yi-yi!' sang Vixen as we shot round the curves. 'Toot-toot-toot!' went the driver's bugle at the dangerous places, and 'Yow! yow! yow!' bayed Garm. Kadir Buksh sat on the front seat and smiled. Even he was glad to get away from the heat of the Plains that stewed in the haze behind us. Now and then we would meet a man we knew going down to his work again, and he would say: 'What's it like below?' and I would shout: 'Hotter than cinders. What's it like up above?' and he would shout back: 'Just perfect!' and away we would go.

Suddenly Kadir Buksh said, over his

shoulder: 'Here is Solon'; and Garm snored where he lay with his head on my knee. Solon is an unpleasant little cantonment, but it has the advantage of being cool and healthy. It is all bare and windy, and one generally stops at a rest-house near by for something to eat. I got out and took both dogs with me, while Kadir Buksh made tea. A soldier told us we should find Stanley 'out there,' nodding his head towards a bare, bleak hill.

When we climbed to the top we spied that very Stanley, who had given me all this trouble, sitting on a rock with his face in his hands and his overcoat hanging loose about him. I never saw anything so lonely and dejected in my life as this one little man, crumpled up and thinking, on the great grey hillside.

Here Garm left me.

He departed without a word, and, so far as I could see, without moving his legs. He flew through the air bodily, and I heard the whack of him as he flung himself at Stanley, knocking the little man clean over. They rolled on the ground together, shouting, and yelping, and hugging. I could not see which was dog and which was man, till Stanley got up and whimpered.

He told me that he had been suffering from fever at intervals, and was very weak. He looked all he said, but even while I watched, both man and dog plumped out to their natural sizes, precisely as dried apples swell in water. Garm was on his shoulder, and his breast and feet all at the same time, so that Stanley spoke all through a cloud of Garm – gulping, sobbing, slavering Garm. He did not say anything that I could understand, except that he had fancied he was going to die, but that now he was quite well, and that he was not going to give up Garm any more to anybody under the rank of Beelzebub.

Then he said he felt hungry, and thirsty, and happy.

We went down to tea at the rest-house, where Stanley stuffed himself with sardines and raspberry jam, and beer, and cold mutton and pickles, when Garm wasn't climbing over him; and then Vixen and I went on.

Garm saw how it was at once. He said goodbye to me three times, giving me both paws one after another, and leaping on to my shoulder. He further escorted us, singing Hosannas at the top of his voice, a mile down the road. Then he raced back to his own master.

Vixen never opened her mouth, but when the cold twilight came, and we could see the lights of Simla across the hills, she snuffled with her nose at the breast of my ulster. I unbuttoned it, and tucked her inside. Then she gave a contented little sniff, and fell fast asleep, her head on my breast, till we bundled out at Simla, two of the four happiest people in all the world that night.

THE WHITE SEAL

Oh! hush thee, my baby, the night is
  behind us,
And black are the waters that sparkled so
  green.
The moon, o'er the combers, looks
  downward to find us
At rest in the hollows that rustle between.
Where billow meets billow, there soft be
  thy pillow;
Ah, weary wee flipperling, curl at thy ease!
The storm shall not wake thee, nor shark
  overtake thee,
Asleep in the arms of the slow-swinging
  seas.

Seal Lullaby.

All these things happened several years ago
at a place called Novastoshnah, or North
East Point, on the Island of St Paul, away
and away in the Bering Sea. Limmershin,
the Winter Wren, told me the tale when he
was blown on to the rigging of a steamer
going to Japan, and I took him down into
my cabin and warmed and fed him for a
couple of days till he was fit to fly back to St
Paul's again. Limmershin is a very odd little

bird, but he knows how to tell the truth.

Nobody comes to Novastoshnah except on business, and the only people who have regular business there are the seals. They come in the summer months by hundreds and hundreds of thousands out of the cold grey sea; for Novastoshnah Beach has the finest accommodation for seals of any place in all the world.

Sea Catch knew that, and every spring would swim from whatever place he happened to be in – would swim like a torpedo-boat straight for Novastoshnah, and spend a month fighting with his companions for a good place on the rocks as close to the sea as possible. Sea Catch was fifteen years old, a huge grey fur-seal with almost a mane on his shoulders, and long, wicked dog-teeth. When he heaved himself up on his front flippers he stood more than four feet clear of the ground, and his weight, if any one had been bold enough to weigh him, was nearly seven hundred pounds. He was scarred all over with the marks of savage fights, but he was always ready for just one fight more. He would put his head on one side, as though he were afraid to look his enemy in the face; then he would shoot it out like lightning, and when the big teeth were firmly fixed on the other seal's neck, the other seal might get away if he could, but Sea Catch would not help him.

Yet Sea Catch never chased a beaten seal, for that was against the Rules of the Beach. He only wanted room by the sea for his nursery; but as there were forty or fifty thousand other seals hunting for the same thing each spring, the whistling, bellowing, roaring, and blowing on the beach were something frightful.

From a little hill called Hutchinson's Hill you could look over three and a half miles of ground covered with fighting seals; and the surf was dotted all over with the heads of seals hurrying to land and begin their share of the fighting. They fought in the breakers, they fought in the sand, and they fought on the smooth-worn basalt rocks of the nurseries; for they were just as stupid and unaccommodating as men. Their wives never came to the island until late in May or early in June, for they did not care to be torn to pieces and the young two-, three-, and four-year-old seals who had not begun housekeeping went inland about half a mile through the ranks of the fighters and played about on the sand-dunes in droves and legions, and rubbed off every single green thing that grew. They were called the holluschickie – the bachelors – and there were perhaps two or three hundred thousand of them at Novastoshnah alone.

Sea Catch had just finished his forty-fifth fight one spring when Matkah, his soft, sleek, gentle-eyed wife, came up out of the sea, and he caught her by the scruff of the neck and dumped her down on his reservation, saying gruffly: 'Late, as usual. Where *have* you been?'

It was not the fashion for Sea Catch to eat anything during the four months he stayed on the beaches, and so his temper was generally bad. Matkah knew better than to answer back. She looked round and cooed: 'How thoughtful of you! You've taken the old place again.'

'I should think I had,' said Sea Catch. 'Look at me!'

He was scratched and bleeding in twenty places; one eye was almost blind, and his sides were torn to ribbons.

'Oh, you men, you men!' Matkah said, fanning herself with her hind flipper. 'Why can't you be sensible and settle your places quietly? You look as though you had been fighting with the Killer Whale.'

'I haven't been doing anything but fight since the middle of May. The beach is disgracefully crowded this season. I've met at least a hundred seals from Lukannon Beach, house-hunting. Why can't people stay where they belong?'

'I've often thought we should be much happier if we hauled out at Otter Island instead of this crowded place,' said Matkah.

'Bah! Only the holluschickie go to Otter

Island. If we went there they would say we were afraid. We must preserve appearances, my dear.'

Sea Catch sunk his head proudly between his fat shoulders and pretended to go to sleep for a few minutes, but all the time he was keeping a sharp look-out for a fight. Now that all the seals and their wives were on the land, you could hear their clamour miles out to sea above the loudest gales. At the lowest counting there were over a million seals on the beach – old seals, mother seals, tiny babies, and holluschickie, fighting, scuffling, bleating, crawling, and playing together – going down to the sea and coming up from it in gangs and regiments, lying over every foot of ground as far as the eye could reach, and skirmishing about in brigades through the fog. It is nearly always foggy at Novastoshnah, except when the sun comes out and makes everything look all pearly and rainbow-coloured for a little while.

Kotick, Matkah's baby, was born in the middle of that confusion, and he was all head and shoulders, with pale, watery-blue eyes, as tiny seals must be; but there was something about his coat that made his mother look at him very closely.

'Sea Catch,' she said at last, 'our baby's going to be white!'

'Empty clam-shells and dry seaweed!' snorted Sea Catch. 'There never has been such a thing in the world as a white seal.'

'I can't help that,' said Matkah; 'there's going to be now'; and she sang the low, crooning seal-song that all the mother seals sing to their babies:

You mustn't swim till you're six weeks old,
Or your head will be sunk by your heels
And summer gales and Killer Whales
Are bad for baby seals.

Are bad for baby seals, dear rat,
As bad as bad can be;
But splash and grow strong,
And you can't be wrong,
Child of the Open Sea!

Of course the little fellow did not understand the words at first. He paddled and scrambled about by his mother's side, and learned to scuffle out of the way when his father was fighting with another seal, and the two rolled and roared up and down the slippery rocks. Matkah used to go to sea to get things to eat, and the baby was fed only once in two days; but then he ate all he could, and throve upon it.

The first thing he did was to crawl inland, and there he met tens of thousands of babies of his own age, and they played together like puppies, went to sleep on the clean sand, and played again. The old people in the nurseries took no notice of them, and the holluschickie kept to their own grounds, so the babies had a beautiful playtime.

When Matkah came back from her deep-sea fishing she would go straight to their playground and call as a sheep calls for a lamb, and wait until she heard Kotick bleat. Then she would take the straightest of straight lines in his direction, striking out with her fore flippers and knocking the youngsters head over heels right and left. There were always a few hundred mothers hunting for their children through the playgrounds, and the babies were kept lively; but, as Matkah told Kotick, 'So long as you don't lie in muddy water and get mange, or rub the hard sand into a cut or scratch, and so long as you never go swimming when there is a heavy sea, nothing will hurt you here.'

Little seals can no more swim than little children, but they are unhappy till they learn. The first time that Kotick went down to the sea a wave carried him out beyond his depth, and his big head sank and his little hind flippers flew up exactly as his mother had told him in the song, and if the next wave had not thrown him back again he would have drowned.

After that he learned to lie in a beach-pool and let the wash of the waves just cover him and lift him up while he paddled, but he always kept his eye open for big waves that might hurt. He was two weeks learning to use his flippers; and all that while he floundered in and out of the water, and coughed and grunted and crawled up the beach and took cat-naps on the sand, and went back again, until at last he found that he truly belonged to the water.

Then you can imagine the times that he had with his companions, ducking under the rollers; or coming in on top of a comber and landing with a swash and a splutter as the big wave went whirling far up the beach; or standing up on his tail and scratching his head as the old people did; or playing 'I'm the King of the Castle' on slippery, weedy rocks that just stuck out of the wash. Now and then he would see a thin fin, like a big shark's fin, drifting along close to shore, and he knew that that was the Killer Whale, the Grampus, who eats young seals when he can get them; and Kotick would head for the beach like an arrow, and the fin would jig off slowly, as if it were looking for nothing at all.

Late in October the seals began to leave St Paul's for the deep sea, by families and tribes, and there was no more fighting over the nurseries, and the holluschickie played anywhere they liked. 'Next year,' said Matkah to Kotick, 'you will be a holluschickie;

but this year you must learn how to catch fish.'

They set out together across the Pacific, and Matkah showed Kotick how to sleep on his back with his flippers tucked down by his side and his little nose just out of the water. No cradle is so comfortable as the long, rocking swell of the Pacific. When Kotick felt his skin tingle all over, Matkah told him he was learning the 'feel of the water,' and that tingly, prickly feelings meant bad weather coming, and he must swim hard and get away.

'In a little time,' she said, 'you'll know where to swim to, but just now we'll follow Sea Pig, the Porpoise, for he is very wise.' A school of porpoises were ducking and tearing through the water, and little Kotick followed them as fast as he could, 'How do you know where to go to?' he panted. The leader of the school rolled his white eyes, and ducked under. 'My tail tingles, youngster,' he said. 'That means there's a gale behind me. Come along! When you're south of the Sticky Water [he meant the Equator], and your tail tingles, that means there's a gale in front of you and you must head north. Come along! The water feels bad here.'

This was one of the very many things that Kotick learned, and he was always learning. Matkah taught him to follow the cod and the halibut along the under-sea banks, and wrench the rockling out of his hole among the weeds; how to skirt the wrecks lying a hundred fathoms below water, and dart like a rifle-bullet in at one port-hole and out at another as the fishes ran; how to dance on the top of the waves when the lightning was racing all over the sky, and wave his flipper politely to the stumpy-tailed Albatross and the Man-of-War Hawk as they went down the wind; how to jump three or four feet clear of the water, like a dolphin, flippers close to the side and tail curved; to leave the flying-fish alone because they are all bony; to take the shoulder-piece out of a cod at full speed ten fathoms deep and never to stop and look at a boat or a ship, but particularly a row-boat. At the end of six months, what Kotick did not know about deep-sea fishing was not worth the knowing, and all that time he never set flipper on dry ground.

One day, however, as he was lying half asleep in the warm water somewhere off the Island of Juan Fernandez, he felt faint and lazy all over, just as human people do when the spring is in their legs, and he remembered the good firm beaches of Novastoshnah seven thousand miles away, the games his companions played, the smell of the sea-weed, the seal roar, and the fighting. That very minute he turned north, swimming steadily, and as he went on he met scores of his mates, all bound for the same place, and they said: 'Greeting, Kotick! This year we are all holluschickie, and we can dance the Fire-dance in the breakers off Lukannon and play on the new grass. But where did you get that coat?'

Kotick's fur was almost pure white now, and though he felt very proud of it, he only said: 'Swim quickly! My bones are aching for the land.' And so they all came to the beaches where they had been born, and heard the old seals, their fathers, fighting in the rolling mist.

That night Kotick danced the Fire-dance with the yearling seals. The sea is full of fire on summer nights all the way down from Novastoshnah to Lukannon, and each seal leaves a wake like burning oil behind him, and a flaming flash when he jumps, and the waves break in great phosphorescent streaks and swirls. Then they went inland to the holluschickie grounds, and rolled up and down in the new wild wheat, and told stories of what they had done while they had been at sea. They talked about the Pacific as boys would talk about a wood that they had been nutting in, and if any one had understood them, he could have gone away and made such a chart of that ocean as never was. The three- and four-year-old holluschickie romped down from Hutchinson's Hill, crying: 'Out of the way, youngsters! The sea is deep, and you don't know all that's in it yet. Wait till you've rounded the Horn. Hi, you yearling, where did you get that white coat?'

'I didn't get it,' said Kotick; 'it grew.' And just as he was going to roll the speaker over, a couple of black-haired men with flat red faces came from behind a sand-dune, and Kotick, who had never seen a man before, coughed and lowered his head. The holluschickie just bundled off a few yards and sat staring stupidly. The men were no less than Kerick Booterin, the chief of the seal-hunters on the island, and Patalamon, his son. They came from the little village not half a mile from the seal-nurseries, and they were deciding what seals they would drive up to the killing-pens (for the seals were driven just like sheep), to be turned into sealskin jackets later on.

'Ho!' said Patalamon. 'Look! There's a white seal!'

Kerick Booterin turned nearly white under his oil and smoke, for he was an Aleut, and Aleuts are not clean people. Then he began to mutter a prayer. 'Don't touch him, Patalamon. There has never been a white seal since – since I was born. Perhaps it is old Zaharrof's ghost. He was lost last year in the big gale.'

'I'm not going near him,' said Patalamon. 'He's unlucky. Do you really think he is old Zaharrof come back? I owe him for some gulls' eggs.'

'Don't look at him,' said Kerick. 'Head off that drove of four-year-olds. The men ought to skin two hundred today, but it's the beginning of the season, and they are new to the work. A hundred will do. Quick!'

Patalamon rattled a pair of seal's shoulder-bones in front of a herd of holluschickie, and they stopped dead, puffing and blowing. Then he stepped near, and the seals began to move, and Kerick headed them inland, and they never tried to get back to their companions. Hundreds and hundreds of thousands of seals watched them being driven, but they went on playing just the same. Kotick was the only one who asked questions, and none of his companions could tell him anything, except that the men always drove seals in that way for six weeks or two months of every year.

'I am going to follow,' he said, and his eyes nearly popped out of his head as he shuffled along in the wake of the herd.

'The white seal is coming after us,' cried Patalamon. 'That's the first time a seal has ever come to the killing-grounds alone.'

'Hsh! Don't look behind you,' said Kerick. 'It is Zaharrof's ghost! I must speak to the priest about this.'

The distance to the killing-grounds was only half a mile, but it took an hour to cover, because if the seals went too fast Kerick knew that they would get heated and then their fur would come off in patches when they were skinned. So they went on very slowly, past Sea-Lion's Neck, past Webster House, till they came to the Salt House just beyond the sight of the seals on the beach. Kotick followed, panting and wondering. He thought that he was at the world's end, but the roar of the seal-nurseries behind him sounded as loud as the roar of a train in a tunnel. Then Kerick sat down on the moss and pulled out a heavy pewter watch and let the drove cool off for thirty minutes, and Kotick could hear the fog-dew dripping from the brim of his cap. Then ten or twelve men, each with an iron-bound club three or four feet long, came up, and Kerick pointed out one or two of the drove that were bitten by their companions or were too hot, and the men kicked those aside with their heavy boots made of the skin of a walrus's throat, and then Kerick said: 'Let go!' and then the men clubbed the seals on the head as fast as they could.

Ten minutes later little Kotick did not recognise his friends any more, for their skins were ripped off from the nose to the hind flippers – whipped off and thrown down on the ground in a pile.

That was enough for Kotick. He turned and galloped (a seal can gallop very swiftly for a short time) back to the sea, his little new moustache bristling with horror. At Sea-Lion's Neck, where the great sea-lions sit on the edge of the surf, he flung himself flipper over head into the cool water, and rocked there, gasping miserably. 'What's here?' said a sea-lion gruffly; for as a rule the sea-lions keep themselves to themselves.

'*Scoochnie! Ochen scoochnie!*' ('I'm lonesome, very lonesome!') said Kotick. 'They're killing *all* the holluschickie on *all* the beaches.'

The sea-lion turned his head, inshore. 'Nonsense!' he said; 'your friends are making as much noise as ever. You must have seen old Kerick polishing off a drove. He's done that for thirty years.'

'It's horrible,' said Kotick, backing water as a wave went over him, and steadying himself with a screw-stroke of his flippers that brought him up all standing within three inches of a jagged edge of rock.

'Well done for a yearling!' said the sea-lion, who could appreciate good swimming. 'I suppose it is rather awful from your way of looking at it; but if you seals will come here year after year, of course the men get to know of it, and unless you can find an island where no men ever come, you will always be driven.

'Isn't there any such island?' began Kotick.

'I've followed the *poltoos* [the halibut] for twenty years, and I can't say I've found it yet. But look here – you seem to have a fondness for talking to your betters; suppose you go to Walrus Islet and talk to Sea Vitch. He may know something. Don't flounce off like that. It's a six-mile swim, and if I were you I should haul out and take a nap first, little one.

Kotick thought that that was good advice, so he swam round to his own beach, hauled out, and slept for half an hour, twitching all over, as seals will. Then he headed straight for Walrus Islet, a little low sheet of rocky island almost due north-east from Novastoshnah, all ledges of rock and gulls' nests, where the walrus herded by themselves.

He landed close to old Sea Vitch – the big, ugly, bloated, pimpled, fat-necked, long-tusked walrus of the North Pacific, who has no manners except when he is asleep – as he was then, with his hind flippers half in and half out of the surf.

'Wake up!' barked Kotick, for the gulls were making a great noise.

'Hah! Ho! Hmph! What's that?' said Sea Vitch, and he struck the next walrus a blow with his tusks and waked him up, and the next struck the next, and so on till they were all awake and staring in every direction but the right one.

'Hi! It's me,' said Kotick, bobbing in the surf and looking like a little white slug.

'Well! May I be skinned!' said Sea Vitch, and they all looked at Kotick as you can fancy a club full of drowsy old gentlemen would look at a little boy. Kotick did not care to hear any more about skinning just then; he had seen enough of it; so he called out: 'Isn't there any place for seals to go where men don't ever come?'

'Go and find out,' said Sea Vitch, shutting his eyes. 'Run away. We're busy here.'

Kotick made his dolphin-jump in the air and shouted as loud as he could: 'Clam-eater! Clam-eater!' He knew that Sea Vitch never caught a fish in his life, but always rooted for clams and seaweeds, though he pretended to be a very terrible person. Naturally the Chickies and the Gooverooskies and the Epatkas, the Burgomaster Gulls and the Kittiwakes and the Puffins, who are always looking for a chance to be rude, took up the cry, and – so Limmershin told me – for nearly five minutes you could not have heard a gun fired on Walrus Islet. All the population was yelling and screaming 'Clam-eater! *Stareek* [old man]!' while Sea Vitch rolled from side to side grunting and coughing.

'*Now* will you tell?' said Kotick, all out of breath.

'Go and ask Sea Cow,' said Sea Vitch. 'If

he is living still, he'll be able to tell you.'

'How shall I know Sea Cow when I meet him?' said Kotick, sheering off.

'He's the only thing in the sea uglier than Sea Vitch,' screamed a Burgomaster Gull, wheeling under Sea Vitch's nose. 'Uglier, and with worse manners! *Stareek!*'

Kotick swam back to Novastoshnah, leaving the gulls to scream. There he found that no one sympathised with him in his little attempts to discover a quiet place for the seals. They told him that men had always driven the holluschickie – it was part of the day's work – and that if he did not like to see ugly things he should not have gone to the killing-grounds. But none of the other seals had seen the killing, and that made the difference between him and his friends. Besides, Kotick was a white seal.

'What you must do,' said old Sea Catch, after he had heard his son's adventures, 'is to grow up and be a big seal like your father, and have a nursery on the beach, and then they will leave you alone. In another five years you ought to be able to fight for yourself.' Even gentle Matkah, his mother, said: 'You will never be able to stop the killing. Go and play in the sea, Kotick.' And Kotick went off and danced the Fire-dance with a very heavy little heart.

That autumn he left the beach as soon as he could, and set off alone because of a notion in his bullet-head. He was going to find Sea Cow, if there was such a person in the sea, and he was going to find a quiet island with good firm beaches for seals to live on, where men could not get at them. So he explored and explored by himself from the North to the South Pacific, swimming as much as three hundred miles in a day and a night. He met with more adventures than can be told, and narrowly escaped being caught by the Basking Shark, and the Spotted Shark, and the Hammerhead, and he met all the untrustworthy ruffians that loaf up and down the seas, and the heavy polite fish, and the scarlet-spotted scallops that are moored in one place for hundreds of years, and grow very proud of it; but he never met Sea Cow, and he never found an island that he could fancy.

If the beach was good and hard, with a slope behind it for seals to play on, there was always the smoke of a whaler on the horizon, boiling down blubber, and Kotick knew what *that* meant. Or else he could see that seals had once visited the island and been killed off, and Kotick knew that where men had come once they would come again.

He picked up with an old stumpy-tailed albatross, who told him that Kerguelen Island was the very place for peace and quiet, and when Kotick went down there he was all but smashed to pieces against some wicked black cliffs in a heavy sleet-storm with lightning and thunder. Yet as he pulled out against the gale he could see that even there had once been a seal-nursery. And so it was in all the other islands that he visited.

Limmershin gave a long list of them, for he said that Kotick spent five seasons exploring, with a four months' rest each year at Novastoshnah, when the holluschickie used to make fun of him and his imaginary islands. He went to the Galapagos, a horrid dry place on the Equator, where he was nearly baked to death; he went to the Georgia Islands, the South Orkneys, Emerald Island, Little Nightingale Island, Gough's Island, Bouvet's Island, the Crossets, and even to a little speck of an island south of the Cape of Good Hope. But everywhere the People of the Sea told him the same things. Seals had come to those islands once upon a time, but men had killed them all off. Even when he swam thousands of miles out of the Pacific, and got to a place called Cape Corrientes (that was when he was coming back from Gough's Island), he found a few hundred mangy seals on a rock, and they told him that men came there too.

That nearly broke his heart, and he headed round the Horn back to his own beaches;

and on his way north he hauled out on an island full of green trees, where he found an old, old seal who was dying, and Kotick caught fish for him, and told him all his sorrows. 'Now,' said Kotick, 'I am going back to Novastoshnah, and if I am driven to the killing-pens with the holluschickie I shall not care.'

The old seal said: 'Try once more. I am the last of the Lost Rookery of Masafuera, and in the days when men killed us by the hundred thousand there was a story on the beaches that some day a white seal would come out of the north and lead the seal people to a quiet place. I am old and I shall never live to see that day, but others will. Try once more.'

And Kotick curled up his moustache (it was a beauty), and said: 'I am the only white seal that has ever been born on the beaches, and I am the only seal, black or white, who ever thought of looking for new islands.'

That cheered him immensely; and when he came back to Novastoshnah that summer, Matkah, his mother, begged him to marry and settle down, for he was no longer a holluschick, but a full-grown sea-catch, with a curly white mane on his shoulders as heavy, as big, and as fierce as his father. 'Give me another season,' he said.

'Remember, Mother, it is always the seventh wave that goes farthest up the beach.'

Curiously enough, there was another seal who thought that she would put off marrying till the next year, and Kotick danced the Fire-dance with her all down Lukannon Beach the night before he set off on his last exploration.

This time he went westward, because he had fallen on the trail of a great shoal of halibut, and he needed at least one hundred pounds of fish a day to keep him in good condition. He chased them till he was tired, and then he curled himself up and went to sleep on the hollows of the ground-swell that sets in to Copper Island. He knew the coast perfectly well, so about midnight, when he felt himself gently bumped on a weed-bed, he said, 'H'm, tide's running strong to-night,' and turning over under water opened his eyes slowly and stretched. Then he jumped like a cat, for he saw huge things nosing about in the shoal water and browsing on the heavy fringes of the weeds.

'By the Great Combers of Magellan!' he said, beneath his moustache. 'Who in the Deep Sea are these people?'

They were like no walrus, sea-lion, seal, bear, whale, shark, fish, squid, or scallop that Kotick had ever seen before. They were between twenty and thirty feet long, and they had no hind flippers, but a shovel-like tail that looked as if it had been whittled out of wet leather. Their heads were the most foolish-looking things you ever saw, and they balanced on the ends of their tails in deep water when they weren't grazing, bowing solemnly to one another and waving their front flippers as a fat man waves his arm.

'Ahem!' said Kotick. 'Good sport, gentlemen?' The big things answered by bowing and waving their flippers like the Frog-Footman. When they began feeding again Kotick saw that their upper lip was split into two pieces that they could twitch apart about a foot and bring together again with a whole bushel of seaweed between the splits. They tucked the stuff into their mouths and chumped solemnly.

'Messy style of feeding, that,' said Kotick. They bowed again, and Kotick began to lose his temper. 'Very good,' he said. 'If you do happen to have an extra joint in your front flipper you needn't show off so. I see you bow gracefully, but I should like to know your names.' The split lips moved and twitched, and the glassy green eyes stared; but they did not speak.

'Well!' said Kotick, 'you're the only people I've ever met uglier than Sea Vitch – and with worse manners.'

Then he remembered in a flash what the Burgomaster Gull had screamed to him when he was a little yearling at Walrus Islet, and he tumbled backward in the water, for he knew that he had found Sea Cow at last.

The sea cows went on schlooping and grazing and chumping in the weed, and Kotick asked them questions in every language that he had picked up in his travels: and the Sea People talk nearly as many languages as human beings. But the Sea Cow did not answer, because Sea Cow cannot talk. He has only six bones in his neck where he ought to have seven, and they say under the sea that that prevents him from speaking even to his companions; but, as you know, he has an extra joint in his fore flipper, and by waving it up and down and about he makes a sort of clumsy telegraphic code.

By daylight Kotick's mane was standing on end and his temper was gone where the dead crabs go. Then the Sea Cow began to travel northward very slowly, stopping to hold absurd bowing councils from time to time, and Kotick followed them, saying to himself: 'People who are such idiots as these are would have been killed long ago if they hadn't found out some safe island; and what is good enough for the Sea Cow is good enough for the Sea Catch. All the same, I wish they'd hurry.'

It was weary work for Kotick. The herd never went more than forty or fifty miles a day, and stopped to feed at night, and kept close to the shore all the time; while Kotick swam round them, and over them, and under them, but he could not hurry them on one half-mile. As they went farther north they held a bowing council every few hours, and Kotick nearly bit off his moustache with impatience till he saw that they were following up a warm current of water, and then he respected them more.

One night they sank through the shiny water – sank like stones – and, for the first time since he had known them, began to swim quickly. Kotick followed, and the pace astonished him, for he never dreamed that Sea Cow was anything of a swimmer. They headed for a cliff by the shore – a cliff that ran down into deep water, and plunged into a dark hole at the foot of it, twenty fathoms under the sea. It was a long, long swim, and Kotick badly wanted fresh air before he was out of the dark tunnel that they led him through.

'My wig!' he said, when he rose, gasping and puffing, into open water at the farther end. 'It was a long dive, but it was worth it.'

The sea cows had separated, and were browsing lazily along the edges of the finest beaches that Kotick had ever seen. There were long stretches of smooth-worn rock running for miles, exactly fitted to make seal-nurseries, and there were playgrounds of hard sand sloping inland behind them, and there were rollers for seals to dance in, and long grass to roll in, and sand-dunes to climb up and down; and, best of all, Kotick knew by the feel of the water, which never deceives a true Sea Catch, that no men had ever come there.

The first thing he did was to assure himself that the fishing was good, and then he swam along the beaches and counted up the delightful low sandy islands half hidden in the beautiful rolling fog. Away to the northward out to sea ran a line of bars and shoals and rocks that would never let a ship come within six miles of the beach; and between the islands and the main land was a stretch of deep water that ran up to the perpendicular cliffs, and somewhere below the cliffs was the mouth of the tunnel.

'It's Novastoshnah over again, but ten times better,' said Kotick. 'Sea Cow must be wiser than I thought. Men can't come down the cliffs, even if there were any men; and the shoals to seaward would knock a ship to splinters. If any place in the sea is safe, this is it.'

He began to think of the seal he had left behind him, but though he was in a hurry to go back to Novastoshnah, he thoroughly explored the new country, so that he would be able to answer all questions.

Then he dived and made sure of the

mouth of the tunnel, and raced through to the southward. No-one but a sea cow or a seal would have dreamed of there being such a place, and when he looked back at the cliffs even Kotick could hardly believe that he had been under them.

He was six days going home, though he was not swimming slowly; and when he hauled out just above Sea-Lion's Neck the first person he met was the seal who had been waiting for him, and she saw by the look in his eyes that he had found his island at last.

But the holluschickie and Sea Catch, his father, and all the other seals, laughed at him when he told them what he had discovered, and a young seal about his own age said: 'This is all very well, Kotick, but you can't come from no one knows where and order us off like this. Remember we've been fighting for our nurseries, and that's a thing you never did. You preferred prowling about in the sea.'

The other seals laughed at this, and the young seal began twisting his head from side to side. He had just married that year, and was making a great fuss about it.

'I've no nursery to fight for,' said Kotick. 'I want only to show you all a place where you will be safe. What's the use of fighting?'

'Oh, if you're trying to back out, of course I've no more to say,' said the young seal, with an ugly chuckle.

'Will you come with me if I win?' said Kotick; and a green light came into his eyes, for he was very angry at having to fight at all.

'Very good,' said the young seal carelessly. '*If* you win, I'll come.'

He had no time to change his mind, for Kotick's head darted out and his teeth sank in the blubber of the young seal's neck. Then he threw himself back on his haunches and hauled his enemy down the beach, shook him, and knocked him over. Then Kotick roared to the seals: 'I've done my best for you these five seasons past. I've found you the island where you'll be safe, but unless your heads are dragged off your silly necks you won't believe. I'm going to teach you now. Look out for yourselves!'

Limmershin told me that never in his life – and Limmershin sees ten thousand big seals fighting every year – never in all his little life did he see anything like Kotick's charge into the nurseries. He flung himself at the biggest sea-catch he could find, caught him by the throat, choked him and bumped him and banged him till he grunted for mercy, and then threw him aside and attacked the next. You see, Kotick had never fasted for four months as the big seals did every year, and his deep-sea swimming-trips kept him in perfect condition, and, best of all, he had never fought before. His curly white mane stood up with rage, and his eyes flamed, and his big dog-teeth glistened, and he was splendid to look at.

Old Sea Catch, his father, saw him tearing past, hauling the grizzled old seals about as though they had been halibut, and upsetting the young bachelors in all directions; and Sea Catch gave one roar and shouted: 'He may be a fool, but he is the best fighter on the Beaches. Don't tackle your father, my son! He's with you!'

Kotick roared in answer, and old Sea Catch waddled in, his moustache on end, blowing like a locomotive, while Matkah and the seal that was going to marry Kotick cowered down and admired their men-folk. It was a gorgeous fight, for the two fought as long as there was a seal that dared lift up his head, and then they paraded grandly up and down the beach side by side, bellowing.

At night, just as the Northern Lights were winking and flashing through the fog, Kotick climbed a bare rock and looked down on the scattered nurseries and the torn and bleeding seals. 'Now,' he said, 'I've taught you your lesson.'

'My wig!' said old Sea Catch, boosting himself up stiffly, for he was fearfully mauled. 'The Killer Whale himself could not have cut them up worse. Son, I'm proud of you, and what's more, *I'll* come with you to your island – if there is such a place.'

'Here you, fat pigs of the sea! Who comes with me to the Sea Cow's tunnel? Answer, or I shall teach you again,' roared Kotick.

There was a murmur like the ripple of the tide all up and down the beaches. 'We will come,' said thousands of tired voices. 'We will follow Kotick, the White Seal.'

Then Kotick dropped his head between his shoulders and shut his eyes proudly. He was not a white seal any more, but red from head to tail. All the same, he would have scorned to look at or touch one of his wounds.

A week later he and his army (nearly ten thousand holluschickie and old seals) went away north to the Sea Cow's tunnel, Kotick leading them, and the seals that stayed at Novastoshnah called them idiots. But next spring, when they all met off the fishing-banks of the Pacific, Kotick's seals told such tales of the new beaches beyond Sea Cow's tunnel that more and more seals left Novastoshnah.

Of course it was not all done at once, for the seals need a long time to turn things over in their minds, but year by year more seals went away from Novastoshnah, and Lukannon, and the other nurseries, to the quiet, sheltered beaches where Kotick sits all the summer through, getting bigger and fatter and stronger each year, while the holluschickie play round him in that sea where no man comes.

THE MALTESE CAT

They had good reason to be proud, and better reason to be afraid, all twelve of them; for, though they had fought their way, game by game, up the teams entered for the polo tournament, they were meeting the Archangels that afternoon in the final match; and the Archangels' men were playing with half-a-dozen ponies apiece. As the game was divided into six quarters of eight minutes each, that meant a fresh pony after every halt. The Skidars' team, even supposing there were no accidents, could only supply one pony for every other change; and two to one is heavy odds. Again, as Shiraz, the grey Syrian, pointed out, they were meeting the pink and pick of the polo ponies of Upper India; ponies that had cost from a thousand rupees each, while they themselves were a cheap lot gathered, often from country carts, by their masters who belonged to a poor but honest native infantry regiment.

'Money means pace and weight,' said Shiraz, rubbing his black silk nose dolefully along his neat-fitting boot, 'and by the maxims of the game as I know it–'

'Ah, but we aren't playing the maxims,' said

the Maltese Cat. 'We're playing the game, and we've the great advantage of knowing the game. Just think a stride, Shiraz. We've pulled up from bottom to second place in two weeks against all those fellows on the ground here; and that's because we play with our heads as well as with our feet.'

'It makes me feel undersized and unhappy all the same,' said Kittiwynk, a mouse-coloured mare with a red browband and the cleanest pair of legs that ever an aged pony owned. 'They've twice our size, these others.'

Kittiwynk looked at the gathering and sighed. The hard, dusty Umballa polo-ground was lined with thousands of soldiers, black and white, not counting hundreds and hundreds of carriages, and drags, and dog-carts, and ladies with brilliant-coloured parasols, and officers in uniform and out of it, and crowds of natives behind them; and orderlies on camels who had halted to watch the game, instead of carrying letters up and down the station, and native horse-dealers running about on thin-eared Biluchi mares, looking for a chance to sell a few first-class polo ponies. Then there were the ponies of thirty teams that had entered for the Upper India Free-for-All Cup – nearly every pony of worth and dignity from Mhow to Peshawar, from Allahabad to Multan; prize ponies, Arabs, Syrian, Barb, country-bred, Deccanee, Waziri, and Kabul ponies of every colour and shape and temper that you could imagine. Some of them were in mat-roofed stables close to the polo-ground, but most were under saddle while their masters, who had been defeated in the earlier games, trotted in and out and told each other exactly how the game should be played.

It was a glorious sight, and the come-and-go of the little quick hoofs, and the incessant salutations of ponies that had met before on other polo-grounds or racecourses, were enough to drive a four-footed thing wild.

But the Skidars' team were careful not to know their neighbours, though half the ponies on the ground were anxious to scrape acquaintance with the little fellows that had come from the North, and, so far, had swept the board.

'Let's see,' said a soft, golden-coloured Arab, who had been playing very badly the day before, to the Maltese Cat, 'didn't we meet in Abdul Rahman's stable in Bombay four seasons ago? I won the Paikpattan Cup next season, you may remember.'

'Not me,' said the Maltese Cat politely. 'I was at Malta then, pulling a vegetable cart. I don't race. I play the game.'

'O-oh!' said the Arab, cocking his tail and swaggering off.

'Keep yourselves to yourselves,' said the Maltese Cat to his companions. 'We don't want to rub noses with all those goose-rumped half-breeds of Upper India. When we've won this cup they'll give their shoes to know us.'

'*We* shan't win the cup,' said Shiraz. 'How do you feel?'

'Stale as last night's feed when a musk-rat has run over it,' said Polaris, a rather heavy-shouldered grey, and the rest of the team agreed with him.

'The sooner you forget that the better,' said the Maltese Cat cheerfully. 'They've finished tiffin in the big tent. We shall be wanted now. If your saddles are not comfy, kick. If your bits aren't easy, rear, and let the *saises* know whether your boots are tight.'

Each pony had his *sais*, his groom, who lived and ate and slept with the pony, and had betted a great deal more than he could afford on the result of the game. There was no chance of anything going wrong, and, to make sure, each *sais* was shampooing the legs of his pony to the last minute. Behind the *saises* sat as many of the Skidars' regiment as had leave to attend the match – about half the native officers, and a hundred or two dark, black-bearded men with the regimental pipers nervously fingering the big be-ribboned bagpipes. The Skidars were what they call a Pioneer regiment; and the bagpipes made the national music of half the men. The native officers held bundles of polo-sticks, long cane-handled mallets, and as the grand-stand filled after lunch they arranged themselves by ones and twos at different points round the ground, so that if a stick were broken the player would not have far to ride for a new one. An impatient British cavalry band struck up 'If you want to know the time, ask a p'leeceman!' and the two umpires in light dust-coats danced out on two little excited ponies. The four players of the Archangels' team followed, and the sight of their beautiful mounts made Shiraz groan again.

'Wait till we know,' said the Maltese Cat. 'Two of 'em are playing in blinkers, and that means they can't see to get out of the way of their own side, or they may shy at the umpires' ponies. They've *all* got white web reins that are sure to stretch or slip!'

'And,' said Kittiwynk, dancing to take the stiffness out of her, 'they carry their whips in their hands instead of on their wrists. Hah!'

'True enough. No man can manage his stick and his reins, and his whip that way,' said the Maltese Cat. 'I've fallen over every square yard of the Malta ground, and *I* ought to know.' He quivered his little flea-bitten withers just to show how satisfied he felt; but his heart was not so light. Ever since he had drifted into India on a troopship, taken, with an old rifle, as part payment for a racing debt, the Maltese Cat had played and preached polo to the

Skidars' team on the Skidars' stony polo-ground. Now a polo pony is like a poet. If he is born with a love for the game he can be made. The Maltese Cat knew that bamboos grew solely in order that polo-balls might be turned from their roots, that grain was given to ponies to keep them in hard condition, and that ponies were shod to prevent them slipping on a turn. But, besides all these things, he knew every trick and device of the finest game of the world, and for two seasons he had been teaching the others all he knew or guessed.

'Remember,' he said for the hundredth time as the riders came up, 'we *must* play together, and you *must* play with your heads. Whatever happens, follow the ball. Who goes out first?'

Kittiwynk, Shiraz, Polaris, and a short high little bay fellow with tremendous hocks and no withers worth speaking of (he was called Corks) were being girthed up, and the soldiers in the background stared with all their eyes.

'I want you men to keep quiet,' said Lutyens, the captain of the team, 'and especially *not* to blow your pipes.'

'Not if we win, Captain Sahib?' asked a piper.

'If we win, you can do what you please,' said Lutyens, with a smile, as he slipped the loop of his stick over his wrist, and wheeled to canter to his place. The Archangels' ponies were a little bit above themselves on account of the many-coloured crowd so close to the ground. Their riders were excellent players, but they were a team of crack players instead of a crack team; and that made all the difference in the world. They honestly meant to play together, but it is very hard for four men, each the best of the team he is picked from, to remember that in polo no brilliancy of hitting or riding makes up for playing alone. Their captain shouted his orders to them by name, and it is a curious thing that if you call his name aloud in public after an Englishman you make him hot and fretty. Lutyens said nothing to his men because it had all been said before. He pulled up Shiraz, for he was playing 'back,' to guard the goal. Powell on Polaris was half-back, and Macnamara and Hughes on Corks and Kittiwynk were forwards. The tough bamboo-root ball was put into the middle of the ground one hundred and fifty yards from the ends, and Hughes crossed sticks, heads-up, with the captain of the Archangels, who saw fit to play forward, and that is a place from which you cannot easily control the team. The little click as the cane-shafts met was heard all over the ground, and then Hughes made some sort of quick wrist-stroke that just dribbled the ball a few yards. Kittiwynk knew that stroke of old, and followed as a cat follows a mouse. While the captain of the Archangels was wrenching his pony round Hughes struck with all his strength, and next instant Kittiwynk was away, Corks following close behind her, their little feet pattering like raindrops on glass.

'Pull out to the left,' said Kittiwynk between her teeth, 'it's coming our way, Corks!'

The back and half-back of the Archangels were tearing down on her just as she was within reach of the ball. Hughes leaned forward with a loose rein, and cut it away to the left almost under Kittiwynk's feet, and it hopped and skipped off to Corks, who saw that, if he were not quick, it would run beyond the boundaries. That long bounding drive gave the Archangels time to wheel and send three men across the ground to head off Corks. Kittiwynk stayed where she was, for she knew the game. Corks was on the ball half a fraction of a second before the others came up, and Macnamara, with a back-handed stroke, sent it back across the ground to Hughes, who saw the way clear to the Archangels' goal, and smacked the ball in before any one quite knew what had happened.

'That's luck,' said Corks, as they changed ends. 'A goal in three minutes for three hits and no riding to speak of.'

'Don't know,' said Polaris. 'We've made 'em angry too soon. Shouldn't wonder if they try to rush us off our feet next time.'

'Keep the ball hanging then,' said Shiraz. 'That wears out every pony that isn't used to it.'

Next time there was no easy galloping across the ground. All the Archangels closed up as one man, but there they stayed, for Corks, Kittiwynk, and Polaris were somewhere on the top of the ball, marking time among the rattling sticks, while Shiraz circled about outside, waiting for a chance.

'*We* can do this all day,' said Polaris, ramming his quarters into the side of another pony. 'Where do you think you're shoving to?'

'I'll – I'll be driven in an *ekka* if I know,' was the gasping reply, 'and I'd give a week's feed to get my blinkers off. I can't see anything.'

'The dust is rather bad. Whew! That was one for my off hock. Where's the ball, Corks?'

'Under my tail. At least a man's looking for it there. This is beautiful. They can't use their sticks, and it's driving 'em wild. Give old blinkers a push and he'll go over!'

'Here, don't touch me! I can't see. I'll – I'll back out, I think,' said the pony in blinkers, who knew that if you can't see all round your head you cannot prop yourself against a shock.

Corks was watching the ball where it lay in the dust close to his near fore, with Macnamara's shortened stick tap-tapping it from time to time. Kittiwynk was edging her way out of the scrimmage, whisking her stump of a tail with nervous excitement.

'Ho! They've got it,' she snorted. 'Let me out!' and she galloped like a rifle-bullet just behind a tall lanky pony of the Archangels, whose rider was swinging up his stick for a stroke.

'Not today, thank you,' said Hughes, as the blow slid off his raised stick, and Kittiwynk laid her shoulder to the tall pony's quarters, and shoved him aside just as Lutyens on Shiraz sent the ball where it had come from, and the tall pony went skating and slipping away to the left. Kittiwynk, seeing that Polaris had joined Corks in the chase for the ball up the ground, dropped into Polaris's place, and then time was called.

The Skidars' ponies wasted no time in kicking or fuming. They knew each minute's rest meant so much gain, and trotted off to the rails and their *saises*, who began to scrape and blanket and rub them at once.

'Whew!' said Corks, stiffening up to get all the tickle out of the big vulcanite scraper. 'If we were playing pony for pony we'd bend those Archangels double in half an hour. But they'll bring out fresh ones and fresh ones, and fresh ones after that – you see.'

'Who cares?' said Polaris.

'We've drawn first blood. Is my hock swelling?'

'Looks puffy,' said Corks. 'You must have had rather a wipe. Don't let it stiffen. You'll be wanted again in half an hour.'

'What's the game like?' said the Maltese Cat.

'Ground's like your shoe, except where they've put too much water on it,' said Kittiwynk. 'Then it's slippery. Don't play in the centre. There's a bog there. I don't know how their next four are going to behave, but we kept the ball hanging and made 'em lather for nothing. Who goes out? Two Arabs and a couple of countrybreds! That's bad. What a comfort it is to wash your mouth out!'

Kitty was talking with the neck of a leather-covered soda-water bottle between her teeth and trying to look over her withers at the same time. This gave her a very coquettish air.

'What's bad?' said Grey Dawn, giving to the girth and admiring his well-set shoulders.

'You Arabs can't gallop fast enough to keep yourselves warm – that's what Kitty means,' said Polaris, limping to show that his hock needed attention. 'Are you playing "back," Grey Dawn?'

'Looks like it,' said Grey Dawn, as Lutyens

125

swung himself up. Powell mounted the Rabbit, a plain bay countrybred much like Corks, but with mulish ears. Macnamara took Faiz Ullah, a handy short-backed little red Arab with a long tail, and Hughes mounted Benami, an old and sullen brown beast, who stood over in front more than a polo pony should.

'Benami looks like business,' said Shiraz. 'How's your temper, Ben?' The old campaigner hobbled off without answering, and the Maltese Cat looked at the new Archangel ponies prancing about on the ground. They were four beautiful blacks, and they saddled big enough and strong enough to eat the Skidars' team and gallop away with the meal inside them.

'Blinkers again,' said the Maltese Cat. 'Good enough!'

'They're chargers – cavalry chargers!' said Kittiwynk indignantly. *They'll* never see thirteen-three again.'

'They've all been fairly measured and they've all got their certificates,' said the Maltese Cat, 'or they wouldn't be here. We must take things as they come along, and keep our eyes on the ball.'

The game began, but this time the Skidars were penned to their own end of the ground, and the watching ponies did not approve of that.

'Faiz Ullah is shirking, as usual,' said

Polaris, with a scornful grunt.

'Faiz Ullah is eating whip,' said Corks. They could hear the leather-thonged polo quirt lacing the little fellow's well-rounded barrel. Then the Rabbit's shrill neigh came across the ground. 'I can't do all the work,' he cried.

'Play the game, don't talk,' the Maltese Cat whickered; and all the ponies wriggled with excitement, and the soldiers and the grooms gripped the railings and shouted. A black pony with blinkers had singled out old Benami, and was interfering with him in every possible way. They could see Benami shaking his head up and down and flapping his underlip.

'There'll be a fall in a minute,' said Polaris. 'Benami is getting stuffy.'

The game flickered up and down between goalpost and goalpost, and the black ponies were getting more confident as they felt they had the legs of the others. The ball was hit out of a little scrimmage, and Benami and the Rabbit followed it; Faiz Ullah only too glad to be quiet for an instant.

The blinkered black pony came up like a hawk, with two of his own side behind him, and Benami's eye glittered as he raced. The question was which pony should make way for the other; each rider was perfectly willing to risk a fall in a good cause. The black who had been driven nearly crazy by his blinkers trusted to his weight and his temper; but Benami knew how to apply his weight and how to keep his temper. They met, and there was a cloud of dust. The black was lying on his side with all the breath knocked out of his body. The Rabbit was a hundred yards up the ground with the ball, and Benami was sitting down. He had slid nearly ten yards, but he had had his revenge, and sat cracking his nostrils till the black pony rose.

'That's what you get for interfering. Do you want any more?' said Benami, and he plunged into the game. Nothing was done because Faiz Ullah would not gallop, though Macnamara beat him whenever he could spare a second. The fall of the black pony had impressed his companions tremendously, and so the Archangels could not profit by Faiz Ullah's bad behaviour.

But as the Maltese Cat said, when time was called and the four came back blowing and dripping, Faiz Ullah ought to have been kicked all round Umballa. If he did not behave better next time, the Maltese Cat promised to pull out his Arab tail by the root and eat it.

There was no time to talk, for the third four were ordered out.

The third quarter of a game is generally the hottest, for each side thinks that the others must be pumped; and most of the winning play in a game is made about that time.

Lutyens took over the Maltese Cat with a pat and a hug, for Lutyens valued him more than anything else in the world. Powell had Shikast, a little grey rat with no pedigree and no manners outside polo; Macnamara mounted Bamboo, the largest of the team, and Hughes took Who's Who, *alias* The Animal. He was supposed to have Australian blood in his veins, but he looked like a clotheshorse, and you could whack him on the legs with an iron crowbar without hurting him.

They went out to meet the very flower of the Archangels' team, and when Who's Who saw their elegantly booted legs and their beautiful satiny skins he grinned a grin through his light, well-worn bridle.

'My word!' said Who's Who. 'We must give 'em a little football. Those gentlemen need a rubbing down.'

'No biting,' said the Maltese Cat warningly, for once or twice in his career Who's Who had been known to forget himself in that way.

'Who said anything about biting? I'm not playing tiddlywinks. I'm playing the game.'

The Archangels came down like a wolf on the fold, for they were tired of football and they wanted polo. They got it more and more. Just after the game began, Lutyens hit a ball that was coming towards him rapidly, and it rose in the air, as a ball sometimes will, with the whirr of a frightened part-ridge. Shikast heard, but could not see it for the minute, though he looked everywhere and up into the air as the Maltese Cat had taught him. When he saw it ahead and overhead, he went forward with Powell as fast as he could put foot to ground. It was then that Powell, a quiet and level-headed man as a rule, became inspired and played a stroke that sometimes comes off success-fully on a quiet afternoon of long practice. He took his stick in both hands, and standing up in his stirrups, swiped at the ball in the air, Munipore fashion. There was one second of paralysed astonishment, and then all four sides of the ground went up in a yell of applause and delight as the ball flew true (you could see the amazed Archangels ducking in their saddles to get out of the line of flight, and looking at it with open mouths), and the regimental pipes of the Skidars squealed from the railings as long as the piper had breath.

Shikast heard the stroke; but he heard the head of the stick fly off at the same time. Nine hundred and ninety-nine ponies out of a thousand would have gone tearing on after the ball with a useless player pulling at their heads, but Powell knew him, and he knew Powell; and the instant he felt Powell's right leg shift a trifle on the saddle-flap he headed to the boundary, where a native officer was frantically waving a new stick. Before the shouts had ended Powell was armed again.

Once before in his life the Maltese Cat had heard that very same stroke played off his own back, and had profited by the confusion it made. This time he acted on experience, and leaving Bamboo to guard the goal in case of accidents, came through the others like a flash, head and tail low, Lutyens standing up to ease him – swept on and on before the other side knew what was the matter, and nearly pitched on his head between the Archangels' goal-posts as Lutyens tipped the ball in after a straight scurry of a hundred and fifty yards. If there was one thing more than another upon which the Maltese Cat prided himself it was on this quick, streaking kind of run half across the ground. He did not believe in taking balls round the field unless you were clearly over-matched. After this they gave the Archangels five minutes' football, and an expensive fast pony hates football because it rumples his temper.

Who's Who showed himself even better than Polaris in this game. He did not permit any wriggling away, but bored joyfully into the scrimmage as if he had his nose in a feed-box, and were looking for something nice. Little Shikast jumped on the ball the minute it got clear, and every time an Archangel pony followed it he found Shikast standing over it asking what was the matter.

'If we can live through this quarter,' said the Maltese Cat, 'I shan't care. Don't take it out of yourselves. Let them do the lathering.'

So the ponies, as their riders explained afterwards, 'shut up.' The Archangels kept them tied fast in front of their goal, but it cost the Archangels' ponies all that was left of their tempers; and ponies began to kick, and men began to repeat compliments, and they chopped at the legs of Who's Who, and he set his teeth and stayed where he was, and the dust stood up like a tree over the scrimmage till that hot quarter ended.

They found the ponies very excited and confident when they went to their *saises*; and the Maltese Cat had to warn them that the worst of the game was coming.

'Now *we* are all going in for the second time,' said he, 'and *they* are trotting out fresh ponies. You'll think you can gallop, but you'll find you can't; and then you'll be sorry.'

'But two goals to nothing is a halter-long lead,' said Kittiwynk prancing.

'How long does it take to get a goal?' the Maltese Cat answered. 'For pity's sake, don't run away with the notion that the game is half-won just because we happen to be in luck now. They'll ride you into the grand-stand if they can; you must *not* give 'em a chance. Follow the ball.'

'Football, as usual?' said Polaris. 'My hock's half as big as a nose-bag.'

'Don't let them have a look at the ball if you can help it. Now leave me alone. I must get all the rest I can before the last quarter.'

He hung down his head and let all his muscles go slack; Shikast, Bamboo, and Who's Who copying his example.

'Better not watch the game,' he said. 'We aren't playing, and we shall only take it out of ourselves if we grow anxious. Look at the ground and pretend it's fly-time.'

They did their best, but it was hard advice to follow. The hoofs were drumming and the sticks were rattling all up and down the ground, and yells of applause from the English troops told that the Archangels were pressing the Skidars hard. The native soldiers behind the ponies groaned and grunted, and said things in undertones, and presently they heard a longdrawn shout and a clatter of hurrahs!

'One to the Archangels,' said Shikast, without raising his head.

'Time's nearly up. Oh, my sire and dam!'

'Faiz Ullah,' said the Maltese Cat, 'if you don't play to the last nail in your shoes this time, I'll kick you on the ground before all the other ponies.'

'I'll do my best when my time comes,' said

the little Arab sturdily.

The *saises* looked at each other gravely as they rubbed their ponies' legs. This was the first time when long purses began to tell, and everybody knew it. Kittiwynk and the others came back with the sweat dripping over their hoofs and their tails telling sad stories.

'They're better than we are,' said Shiraz. 'I knew how it would be.'

'Shut your big head,' said the Maltese Cat; 'we've one goal to the good yet.'

'Yes, but it's two Arabs and two country-breds to play now,' said Corks. 'Faiz Ullah, remember?' He spoke in a biting voice.

As Lutyens mounted Grey Dawn he looked at his men, and they did not look pretty. They were covered with dust and sweat in streaks. Their yellow boots were almost black, their wrists were red and lumpy, and their eyes seemed two inches deep in their heads, but the expression in the eyes was satisfactory.

'Did you take anything at tiffin?' said Lutyens, and the team shook their heads. They were too dry to talk.

'All right. The Archangels did. They are worse pumped than we are.'

'They've got the better ponies,' said Powell. 'I shan't be sorry when this business is over.'

That fifth quarter was a sad one in every

way. Faiz Ullah played like a little red demon; and the Rabbit seemed to be everywhere at once, and Benami rode straight at anything and everything that came in his way, while the umpires on their ponies wheeled like gulls outside the shifting game. But the Archangels had the better mounts – they had kept their racers till late in the game – and never allowed the Skidars to play football. They hit the ball up and down the width of the ground till Benami and the rest were outpaced. Then they went forward, and time and again Lutyens and Grey Dawn were just, and only just, able to send the ball away with a long splitting backhander. Grey Dawn forgot that he was an Arab; and turned from grey to blue as he galloped. Indeed, he forgot too well, for he did not keep his eyes on the ground as an Arab should, but stuck out his nose and scuttled for the dear honour of the game. They had watered the ground once or twice between the quarters, and a careless waterman had emptied the last of his skinful all in one place near the Skidars' goal. It was close to the end of play, and for the tenth time Grey Dawn was bolting after a ball when his near hind foot slipped on the greasy mud and he rolled over and over, pitching Lutyens just clear of the goalpost; and the triumphant Archangels made their goal. Then time was called – two goals all;

but Lutyens had to be helped up, and Grey Dawn rose with his near hind leg strained somewhere.

'What's the damage?' said Powell, his arm round Lutyens.

'Collar-bone, of course,' said Lutyens between his teeth. It was the third time he had broken it in two years, and it hurt him.

Powell and the others whistled. 'Game's up,' said Hughes.

'Hold on. We've five good minutes yet, and it isn't my right hand,' said Lutyens. 'We'll stick it out.'

'I say,' said the captain of the Archangels, trotting up. 'Are you hurt, Lutyens? We'll wait if you care to put in a substitute. I wish – I mean – the fact is, you fellows deserve this game if any team does. Wish we could give you a man or some of our ponies – or something.'

'You're awfully good, but we'll play it to a finish, I think.'

The captain of the Archangels stared for a little. 'That's not half bad,' he said, and went back to his own side, while Lutyens borrowed a scarf from one of his native officers and made a sling of it. Then an Archangel galloped up with a big bath-sponge and advised Lutyens to put it under his arm-pit to ease his shoulder, and between them they tied up his left arm scientifically, and one of the native officers leaped forward with four long glasses that fizzed and bubbled.

The team looked at Lutyens piteously, and he nodded. It was the last quarter, and nothing would matter after that. They drank out the dark golden drink, and wiped their moustaches, and things looked more hopeful.

The Maltese Cat had put his nose into the front of Lutyens' shirt, and was trying to say how sorry he was.

'He knows,' said Lutyens, proudly. 'The beggar knows. I've played him without a bridle before now – for fun.'

'It's no fun now,' said Powell. 'But we haven't a decent substitute.'

'No,' said Lutyens. 'It's the last quarter, and we've got to make our goal and win. I'll trust the Cat.'

'If you fall this time you'll suffer a little,' said Macnamara.

'I'll trust the Cat,' said Lutyens.

'You hear that?' said the Maltese Cat proudly to the others. 'It's worthwhile playing polo for ten years to have that said of you. Now then, my sons, come along. We'll kick up a little bit just to show the Archangels *this* team haven't suffered.'

And, sure enough, as they went on to the ground the Maltese Cat, after satisfying himself that Lutyens was home in the saddle, kicked out three or four times, and Lutyens laughed. The reins were caught up anyhow in the tips of his strapped hand, and he never pretended to rely on them. He knew the Cat would answer to the least pressure of the leg, and by way of showing off – for his shoulder hurt him very much – he bent the little fellow in a close figure-of-eight in and out between the goal-posts. There was a roar from the native officers and men, who dearly loved a piece of *dugabashi* (horsetrick work), as they called it, and the pipes very quietly and scornfully droned out the first bars of a common bazaar-tune called 'Freshly Fresh and Newly New,' just as a warning to the other regiments that the Skidars were fit. All the natives laughed.

'And now,' said the Cat, as they took their place, 'remember that this is the last quarter, and follow the ball!'

'Don't need to be told,' said Who's Who.

'Let me go on. All those people on all four sides will begin to crowd in – just as they did at Malta. You'll hear people calling out, and moving forward and being pushed back, and that is going to make the Archangel ponies very unhappy. But if a ball is struck to the boundary, you go after it, and let the people get out of your way. I went over the pole of a four-in-hand once, and picked a game out of the dust by it. Back me up when I run, and follow the ball.'

There was a sort of an all-round sound of

sympathy and wonder as the last quarter opened, and then there began exactly what the Maltese Cat had foreseen. People crowded in close to the boundaries, and the Archangels' ponies kept looking sideways at the narrowing space. If you know how a man feels to be cramped at tennis – not because he wants to run out of the court, but because he likes to know that he can at a pinch – you will guess how ponies must feel when they are playing in a box of human beings.

'I'll bend some of those men if I can get away,' said Who's Who, as he rocketed behind the ball; and Bamboo nodded without speaking. They were playing the last ounce in them, and the Maltese Cat had left the goal undefended to join them. Lutyens gave him every order that he could to bring him back, but this was the first time in his career that the little wise grey had ever played polo on his own responsibility, and he was going to make the most of it.

'What are you doing here?' said Hughes, as the Cat crossed in front of him and rode off an Archangel.

'The Cat's in charge – mind the goal!' shouted Lutyens, and bowing forward hit the ball full, and followed on, forcing the Archangels towards their own goal.

'No football,' said the Cat. 'Keep the ball by the boundaries and cramp 'em. Play open order and drive 'em to the boundaries.'

Across and across the ground in big diagonals flew the ball, and whenever it came to a flying rush and a stroke close to the boundaries the Archangel ponies moved stiffly. They did not care to go headlong at a wall of men and carriages, though if the ground had been open they could have turned on a sixpence.

'Wriggle her up the sides,' said the Cat. 'Keep her close to the crowd. They hate the carriages. Shikast, keep her up this side.'

Shikast with Powell lay left and right behind the uneasy scuffle of an open scrimmage, and every time the ball was hit away Shikast galloped on it at such an angle that Powell was forced to hit it towards the boundary; and when the crowd had been driven away from that side, Lutyens would send the ball over to the other side and Shikast would slide desperately after it till his friends came down to help. It was billiards, and no football, this time – billiards in a corner pocket; and the cues were not well chalked.

'If they get us out in the middle of the ground they'll walk away from us. Dribble her along the sides,' cried the Cat.

So they dribbled all along the boundary, where a pony could not come on their right-hand side; and the Archangels were furious, and the umpires had to neglect the game to shout at the people to get back, and several blundering mounted policemen tried to restore order, all close to the scrimmage, and the nerves of the Archangels' ponies stretched and broke like cobwebs.

Five or six times an Archangel hit the ball up into the middle of the ground, and each time the watchful Shikast gave Powell his chance to send it back, and after each return, when the dust had settled, men could see that the Skidars had gained a few yards.

Every now and again there were shouts of ''Side! Off side!' from the spectators; but the teams were too busy to care, and the umpires had all they could do to keep their maddened ponies clear of the scuffle.

At last Lutyens missed a short easy stroke, and the Skidars had to fly back helter-skelter to protect their own goal, Shikast leading. Powell stopped the ball with a backhander when it was not fifty yards from the goal-posts, and Shikast spun round with a wrench that nearly hoisted Powell out of his saddle.

'Now's our last chance,' said the Cat, wheeling like a cockchafer on a pin. 'We've got to ride it out. Come along.'

Lutyens felt the little chap take a deep breath, and, as it were, crouch under his rider. The ball was hopping towards the right-hand boundary, an Archangel riding for it with both spurs and a whip; but neither spur nor whip would make his pony stretch himself as he neared the crowd. The Maltese Cat glided under his very nose, picking up his hind legs sharp, for there was not a foot to spare between his quarters and the other pony's bit. It was as neat an exhibition as fancy figure-skating. Lutyens hit with all the strength he had left, but the stick slipped a little in his hand, and the ball flew off to the left instead of keeping close to the boundary. Who's Who was far across the ground, thinking hard as he galloped. He repeated, stride for stride, the Cat's manoeuvres with another Archangel pony, nipping the ball away from under his bridle, and clearing his opponent by half a fraction of an inch, for Who's Who was clumsy behind. Then he drove away towards the right as the Maltese Cat came up from the left; and Bamboo held a middle course exactly between them. The three were making a sort of Government-broad-arrow-shaped attack; and there was only the Archangels' back to guard the goal; but immediately behind them were three Archangels racing all they knew, and mixed up with them was Powell, sending Shikast along on what he felt was their last hope. It takes a very good man to stand up to the rush of seven crazy ponies in the last quarter of a cup game, when men are riding with their necks for sale, and the ponies are delirious. The Archangels' back missed his stroke, and pulled aside just in time to let the rush go by. Bamboo and Who's Who shortened stride to give the Maltese Cat room, and Lutyens got the goal with a clean, smooth, smacking stroke that was heard all over the field. But there was no stopping the ponies. They poured through the goal-posts in one mixed mob, winners and losers together, for the pace had been terrific. The Maltese Cat knew by experience what would happen, and, to save Lutyens, turned to the right with one last effort that strained a back-sinew beyond hope of repair. As he did so he heard the right-hand goal-post crack as a pony cannoned into it – crack, splinter, and fall like a mast. It had been sawed three parts through in case of accidents, but it upset the pony nevertheless, and he blundered into another, who blundered into the left-hand post, and then there was confusion and dust and wood. Bamboo was lying on the ground, seeing stars; an Archangel pony rolled beside him, breathless and angry; Shikast had sat down dog-fashion to avoid falling over the others, and was sliding along on his little bobtail in a cloud of dust; and Powell was sitting on the ground, hammering with his stick and trying to cheer. All the others were shouting at the top of what was left of their voices, and the men who had been spilt were shouting too. As soon as the people saw no one was hurt, ten thousand native and English shouted and clapped and yelled, and before any one could stop them the pipers of the Skidars broke on to the ground, with all the native officers and men behind them, and marched up and down, playing a wild northern tune called 'Zakhme Bagân,' and through the insolent blaring of the pipes and the high-pitched native yells you could hear the Archangels' band hammering 'For they are all jolly good fellows,' and then reproachfully to the losing team, 'Ooh, Kafoozalum! Kafoozalum! Kafoozalum!'

Besides all these things and many more, there was a Commander-in-Chief, and an Inspector-General of Cavalry, and the principal veterinary officer in all India, standing on the top of a regimental coach, yelling like schoolboys; and brigadiers and colonels and commissioners, and hundreds of pretty ladies joined the chorus. But the Maltese Cat stood with his head down, wondering how many legs were left to him; and Lutyens watched the men and ponies pick themselves out of the wreck of the two goal-posts, and he patted the Cat very tenderly.

'I say,' said the captain of the Archangels, spitting a pebble out of his mouth, 'will you

144

take three thousand for that pony – as he stands?'

'No, thank you. I've an idea he's saved my life,' said Lutyens, getting off and lying down at full length. Both teams were on the ground too, waving their boots in the air, and coughing and drawing deep breaths, as the *saises* ran up to take away the ponies, and an officious water-carrier sprinkled the players with dirty water till they sat up.

'My Aunt!' said Powell, rubbing his back and looking at the stumps of the goal-posts, 'that was a game!'

They played it over again, every stroke of it, that night at the big dinner, when the Free-for-All Cup was filled and passed down the table, and emptied and filled again, and everybody made most eloquent speeches. About two in the morning, when there might have been some singing, a wise little, plain little, grey little head looked in through the open door.

'Hurrah! Bring him in,' said the Archangels; and his *sais*, who was very happy indeed, patted the Maltese Cat on the flank, and he limped in to the blaze of light and the glittering uniforms, looking for Lutyens. He was used to messes and men's bedrooms, and places where ponies are not usually encouraged, and in his youth had jumped on and off a mess-table for a bet. So he behaved himself very politely, and ate bread dipped in salt, and was petted all round the table, moving gingerly; and they drank his health, because he had done more to win the Cup than any man or horse on the ground.

That was glory and honour enough for the rest of his days, and the Maltese Cat did not complain much when his veterinary surgeon said that he would be no good for polo any more. When Lutyens married, his wife did not allow him to play, so he was forced to be an umpire; and his pony on these occasions was a flea-bitten grey with a neat polo-tail, lame all round, but desperately quick on his feet, and, as everybody knew, Past Pluperfect Prestissimo Player of the Game.

LUKANNON

This is the great deep-sea song that all the St Paul seals sing when they are heading back to beaches in the summer. It is a sort of very sad seal National Anthem.

I met my mates in the morning (and oh,
　but I am old!)
Where roaring on the ledges the summer
　ground-swell rolled;
I heard them lift the chorus that drowned
　the breakers' song –
The Beaches of Lukannon – two million
　voices strong!

*The song of pleasant stations beside the salt
　lagoons,*
*The song of blowing squadrons that shuffled
　down the dunes,*
*The song of midnight dances that churned the
　sea to flame –*
*The Beaches of Lukannon – before the sealers
　came!*

I met my mates in the morning (I'll never
　meet them more!);
They came and went in legions that

darkened all the shore.
And through the foam-flecked offing as far
as voice could reach
We hailed the landing-parties and we sang
them up the beach.

The Beaches of Lukannon – the winter-wheat
so tall –
The dripping, crinkled lichens, and the sea-fog
drenching all!
The platforms of our playground, all shining
smooth and worn!
The Beaches of Lukannon – the home where
we were born!

I meet my mates in the morning, a broken,
scattered band.
Men shoot us in the water and club us on
the land;
Men drive us to the Salt House like silly
sheep and tame,
And still we sing Lukannon – before the
sealers came.

Wheel down, wheel down to southward! Oh,
Gooverooska go!
And tell the Deep-Sea viceroys the story of our
woe;
Ere, empty as the shark's egg the tempest flings
ashore,
The Beaches of Lukannon shall know their
sons no more!

HOW FEAR CAME

The stream is shrunk – the pool is dry,
And we be comrades, thou and I;
With fevered jowl and dusty flank
Each jostling each along the bank;
And by one drouthy fear made still,
Forgoing thought of quest or kill.
Now 'neath his dam the fawn may see
The lean Pack-wolf as cowed as he,
And the tall buck, unflinching, note
The fangs that tore his father's throat.
The pools are shrunk – the streams are dry,
And we be playmates, thou and I,
Till yonder cloud – Good Hunting! – loose
The rain that breaks our Water Truce.

The Law of the Jungle – which is by far the oldest law in the world – has arranged for almost every kind of accident that may befall the Jungle People, till now its code is as perfect as time and custom can make it. You will remember that Mowgli spent a great part of his life in the Seeonee Wolf-Pack, learning the Law from Baloo, the Brown Bear; and it was Baloo who told him, when the boy grew impatient at the constant orders, that the Law was like the

149

Giant Creeper, because it dropped across everyone's back and no one could escape. 'When thou hast lived as long as I have, Little Brother, thou wilt see how all the Jungle obeys at least one Law. And that will be no pleasant sight,' said Baloo.

This talk went in at one ear and out at the other, for a boy who spends his life eating and sleeping does not worry about anything till it actually stares him in the face. But, one year, Baloo's words came true, and Mowgli saw all the Jungle working under the Law.

It began when the winter Rains failed almost entirely, and Ikki, the Porcupine, meeting Mowgli in a bamboo-thicket, told him that the wild yams were drying up. Now everybody knows that Ikki is ridiculously fastidious in his choice of food, and will eat nothing but the very best and ripest. So Mowgli laughed and said, 'What is that to me?'

'Not much *now*,' said Ikki, rattling his quills in a stiff, uncomfortable way, 'but later we shall see. Is there any more diving into the deep rock-pool below the Bee-Rocks, Little Brother?'

'No. The foolish water is going all away, and I do not wish to break my head,' said Mowgli, who, in those days, was quite sure that he knew as much as any five of the Jungle People put together.

'That is thy loss. A small crack might let in

some wisdom.' Ikki ducked quickly to prevent Mowgli from pulling his nose-bristles, and Mowgli told Baloo what Ikki had said. Baloo looked very grave, and mumbled half to himself: 'If I were alone I would change my hunting-grounds now, before the others began to think. And yet – hunting among strangers ends in fighting; and they might hurt the Man-cub. We must wait and see how the *mohwa* blooms.'

That spring the *mohwa* tree, that Baloo was so fond of, never flowered. The greeny, cream-coloured, waxy blossoms were heat-killed before they were born, and only a few bad-smelling petals came down when he stood on his hind legs and shook the tree. Then, inch by inch, the untempered heat crept into the heart of the Jungle, turning it yellow, brown, and at last black. The green growths in the sides of the ravines burned up to broken wires and curled films of dead stuff; the hidden pools sank down and caked over, keeping the last least footmark on their edges as if it had been cast in iron; the juicy-stemmed creepers fell away from the trees they clung to and died at their feet; the bamboos withered, clanking when the hot winds blew, and the moss peeled off the rocks deep in the Jungle, till they were as bare and as hot as the quivering blue boulders in the bed of the stream.

The birds and the monkey-people went

north early in the year, for they knew what was coming; and the deer and the wild pig broke far away to the perished fields of the villages, dying sometimes before the eyes of men too weak to kill them. Chil, the Kite, stayed and grew fat, for there was a great deal of carrion, and evening after evening he brought the news to the beasts, too weak to force their way to fresh hunting-grounds, that the sun was killing the Jungle for three days' flight in every direction.

Mowgli, who had never known what real hunger meant, fell back on stale honey, three years old, scraped out of deserted rock-hives – honey black as a sloe, and dusty with dried sugar. He hunted, too, for deep-boring grubs under the bark of the trees, and robbed the wasps of their new broods. All the game in the Jungle was no more than skin and bone, and Bagheera could kill thrice in a night, and hardly get a full meal. But the want of water was the worst, for though the Jungle People drink seldom they must drink deep.

And the heat went on and on, and sucked up all the moisture, till at last the main channel of the Waingunga was the only stream that carried a trickle of water between its dead banks; and when Hathi, the wild elephant, who lives for a hundred years and more, saw a long, lean blue ridge of rock show dry in the very centre of the stream, he knew that he was looking at the Peace Rock, and then and there he lifted up his trunk and proclaimed the Water Truce, as his father before him had proclaimed it fifty years ago. The deer, wild pig, and buffalo took up the cry hoarsely; and Chil, the Kite, flew in great circles far and wide, whistling and shrieking the warning.

By the Law of the Jungle it is death to kill at the drinking-places when once the Water Truce has been declared. The reason of this is that drinking comes before eating. Every one in the Jungle can scramble along somehow when only game is scarce; but water is water; and when there is but one source of supply, all hunting stops while the Jungle People go there for their needs. In good seasons, when water was plentiful, those who came down to drink at the Waingunga – or anywhere else, for that matter – did so at the risk of their lives, and that risk made no small part of the fascination of the night's doings. To move down so cunningly that never a leaf stirred; to wade knee-deep in the roaring shallows that drown all noise from behind; to drink, looking backward over one shoulder, every muscle ready for the first desperate bound of keen terror; to roll on the sandy margin, and return, wet-muzzled and well plumped out, to the admiring herd, was a thing that all tall-antlered young bucks took a delight in, precisely because they knew that at any moment Bagheera or Shere Khan might leap upon them and bear them down. But now all that life-and-death fun was ended, and the Jungle People came up, starved and weary, to the shrunken river, – tiger, bear, deer, buffalo, and pig, all together, – drank the fouled waters, and hung above them, too exhausted to move off.

The deer and the pig had tramped all day in search of something better than dried bark and withered leaves. The buffaloes had found no wallows to be cool in, and no green crops to steal. The snakes had left the Jungle and come down to the river in the hope of finding a stray frog. They curled round wet stones, and never offered to strike when the nose of a rooting pig dislodged them. The river-turtles had long ago been killed by Bagheera, cleverest of hunters, and the fish had buried themselves deep in the dry mud. Only the Peace Rock lay across the shallows like a long snake, and the little tired ripples hissed as they dried on its hot side.

It was here that Mowgli came nightly for the cool and the companionship. The most hungry of his enemies would hardly have cared for the boy then. His naked hide made him seem more lean and wretched than any of his fellows. His hair was bleached to tow colour by the sun; his ribs stood out like the ribs of a basket, and the lumps on his knees and elbows, where he was used to track on all fours, gave his shrunken limbs the look of knotted grass-stems. But his eye, under his matted forelock, was cool and quiet, for Bagheera was his adviser in this time of trouble, and told him to go quietly, hunt slowly, and never, on any account, to lose his temper.

'It is an evil time,' said the Black Panther, one furnace-hot evening, 'but it will go if we can live till the end. Is thy stomach full, Man-cub?'

'There is stuff in my stomach, but I get no good of it. Think you, Bagheera, the Rains have forgotten us and will never come again?'

'Not I! We shall see the *mohwa* in blossom yet, and the little fawns all fat with new grass. Come down to the Peace Rock and hear the news. On my back, Little Brother.'

'This is no time to carry weight. I can still stand alone, but – indeed we be no fatted bullocks, we two.'

Bagheera looked along his ragged, dusty flank and whispered: 'Last night I killed a bullock under the yoke. So low was I brought that I think I should not have dared to spring if he had been loose. *Wou!*'

Mowgli laughed. 'Yes, we be great hunters now,' said he. 'I am very bold – to eat grubs,' and the two came down together through the crackling undergrowth to the river-bank and the lace-work of shoals that ran out from it in every direction,

'The water cannot live long,' said Baloo, joining them. 'Look across. Yonder are trails like the roads of Man.'

On the level plain of the farther bank the stiff jungle-grass had died standing, and, dying, had mummied. The beaten tracks of the deer and the pig, all heading toward the river, had striped that colourless plain with dusty gullies driven through the ten-foot grass, and, early as it was, each long avenue was full of first-comers hastening to the water. You could hear the does and fawns coughing in the snuff-like dust.

Up-stream, at the bend of the sluggish pool round the Peace Rock, and Warden of the Water Truce, stood Hathi, the wild elephant, with his sons, gaunt and grey in the moonlight, rocking to and fro – always rocking. Below him a little were the van-guard of the deer; below these, again, the pig and the wild buffalo; and on the opposite bank, where the tall trees came down to the water's edge, was the place set apart for the Eaters of Flesh – the tigers, the wolves, the panther, the bear, and the others.

'We are under one Law, indeed,' said Bag-heera, wading into the water and looking across at the lines of clicking horns and starting eyes where the deer and the pig pushed each other to and fro. 'Good hunting, all you of my blood,' he added, lying down at full length, one flank thrust out of the shallows; and then, between his teeth, 'But for that which is the Law it would be *very* good hunting.'

The quick-spread ears of the deer caught the last sentence, and a frightened whisper ran along the ranks. 'The Truce! Remember the Truce!'

'Peace there, peace!' gurgled Hathi, the wild elephant. 'The Truce holds, Bagheera. This is no time to talk of hunting.'

'Who should know better than I?' Bagheera answered, rolling his yellow eyes upstream. 'I am an eater of turtles – a fisher of frogs. *Ngaayah!* Would I could get good from chewing branches!'

'*We* wish so, very greatly,' bleated a young fawn, who had only been born that spring, and did not at all like it. Wretched as the Jungle People were, even Hathi could not help chuckling; while Mowgli, lying on his elbows in the warm water, laughed aloud, and beat up the scum with his feet.

'Well spoken, little bud-horn,' Bagheera purred. 'When the Truce ends that shall be remembered in thy favour,' and he looked keenly through the darkness to make sure of recognising the fawn again.

Gradually the talking spread up and down

the drinking-places. One could hear the scuffling, snorting pig asking for more room; the buffaloes grunting among themselves as they lurched out across the sand-bars, and the deer telling pitiful stories of their long foot-sore wanderings in quest of food. Now and again they asked some question of the Eaters of Flesh across the river, but all the news was bad, and the roaring hot wind of the Jungle came and went between the rocks and the rattling branches, and scattered twigs and dust on the water.

'The men-folk, too, they die beside their ploughs,' said a young sambhur. 'I passed three between sunset and night. They lay still, and their bullocks with them. We also shall lie still in a little.'

'The river has fallen since last night,' said Baloo. 'O Hathi, hast thou ever seen the like of this drought?'

'It will pass, it will pass,' said Hathi, squirting water along his back and sides.

'We have one here that cannot endure long,' said Baloo; and he looked toward the boy he loved.

'I?' said Mowgli indignantly, sitting up in the water. 'I have no long fur to cover my bones, but – but if *thy* hide were taken off, Baloo–'

Hathi shook all over at the idea, and Baloo said severely, 'Man-cub, that is not seemly to tell a Teacher of the Law. *Never* have I been seen without my hide.'

'Nay, I meant no harm, Baloo; but only that thou art, as it were, like the cocoanut in the husk, and I am the same cocoanut all naked. Now that brown husk of thine–' Mowgli was sitting cross-legged, and explaining things with his forefinger in his usual way, when Bagheera put out a paddy paw and pulled him over backward into the water.

'Worse and worse,' said the Black Panther, as the boy rose spluttering. 'First Baloo is to be skinned, and now he is a cocoanut. Be careful that he does not do what the ripe cocoanuts do.'

'And what is that?' said Mowgli, off his guard for the minute, though that is one of the oldest catches in the Jungle.

'Break thy head,' said Bagheera quietly, pulling him under again.

'It is not good to make a jest of thy teacher,' said the bear, when Mowgli had been ducked for the third time.

'Not good! What would ye have? That naked thing running to and fro makes a monkey-jest of those who have once been good hunters, and pulls the best of us by the whiskers for sport.' This was Shere Khan, the Lame Tiger, limping down to the water. He waited a little to enjoy the sensation he made among the deer on the opposite bank;

then he dropped his square, frilled head and began to lap, growling: 'The Jungle has become a whelping-ground for naked cubs now. Look at me, Man-cub!'

Mowgli looked – stared, rather – as insolently as he knew how, and in a minute Shere Khan turned away uneasily. 'Man-cub this, and Man-cub that,' he rumbled, going on with his drink, 'the cub is neither man nor cub, or he would have been afraid. Next season I shall have to beg his leave for a drink. *Augrh!*'

'That may come, too,' said Bagheera, looking him steadily between the eyes. 'That may come, too – Faugh, Shere Khan! – what new shame hast thou brought here?'

The Lame Tiger had dipped his chin and jowl in the water, and dark, oily streaks were floating from it downstream.

'Man!' said Shere Khan coolly. 'I killed an hour since.' He went on purring and growling to himself.

The line of beasts shook and wavered to and fro, and a whisper went up that grew to a cry: 'Man! Man! He has killed Man!' Then all looked towards Hathi, the wild elephant, but he seemed not to hear. Hathi never does anything till the time comes, and that is one of the reasons why he lives so long.

'At such a season as this to kill Man! Was no other game afoot?' said Bagheera scornfully, drawing himself out of the tainted

160

water, and shaking each paw, cat-fashion, as he did so.

'I killed for choice – not for food.' The horrified whisper began again, and Hathi's watchful little white eye cocked itself in Shere Khan's direction. 'For choice,' Shere Khan drawled. 'Now come I to drink and make me clean again. Is there any to forbid?'

Bagheera's back began to curve like a bamboo in a high wind, but Hathi lifted up his trunk and spoke quietly.

'Thy kill was from choice?' he asked; and when Hathi asks a question it is best to answer.

'Even so. It was my right and my Night. Thou knowest, O Hathi.' Shere Khan spoke almost courteously.

'Yes, I know,' Hathi answered; and, after a little silence, 'Hast thou drunk thy fill?'

'For tonight, yes.'

'Go, then. The river is to drink, and not to defile. None but the Lame Tiger would so have boasted of his right at this season when – when we suffer together – Man and Jungle People alike. Clean or unclean, get to thy lair, Shere Khan!'

The last words rang out like silver trumpets, and Hathi's three sons rolled forward half a pace, though there was no need. Shere Khan slunk away, not daring to growl, for he knew – what every one else knows – that when the last comes to the last,

Hathi is the Master of the Jungle.

'What is this right Shere Khan speaks of?' Mowgli whispered in Bagheera's ear. 'To kill Man is *always* shameful. The Law says so. And yet Hathi says –'

'Ask him. I do not know, Little Brother. Right or no right, if Hathi had not spoken I would have taught that lame butcher his lesson. To come to the Peace Rock fresh from a kill of Man – and to boast of it – is a jackal's trick. Besides, he tainted the good water.'

Mowgli waited for a minute to pick up his courage, because no one cared to address Hathi directly, and then he cried: 'What is Shere Khan's right, O Hathi?' Both banks echoed his words, for all the People of the Jungle are intensely curious, and they had just seen something that none, except Baloo, who looked very thoughtful, seemed to understand.

'It is an old tale,' said Hathi; 'a tale older than the Jungle. Keep silence along the banks, and I will tell that tale.'

There was a minute or two of pushing and shouldering among the pigs and the buffalo, and then the leaders of the herds grunted, one after another, 'We wait,' and Hathi strode forward till he was nearly knee-deep in the pool by the Peace Rock. Lean and wrinkled and yellow-tusked though he was, he looked what the Jungle knew him to be –

their master.

'Ye know, children,' he began, 'that of all things ye most fear Man'; and there was a mutter of agreement.

'This tale touches thee, Little Brother,' said Bagheera to Mowgli.

'I? I am of the Pack – a hunter of the Free People,' Mowgli answered. 'What have I to do with Man?'

'And ye do not know why ye fear Man?' Hathi went on. 'This is the reason. In the beginning of the Jungle, and none know when that was, we of the Jungle walked together, having no fear of one another. In those days there was no drought, and leaves and flowers and fruit grew on the same tree, and we ate nothing at all except leaves and flowers and grass and fruit and bark.'

'I am glad I was not born in those days,' said Bagheera. 'Bark is only good to sharpen claws.'

'And the Lord of the Jungle was Tha, the First of the Elephants. He drew the Jungle out of deep waters with his trunk; and where he made furrows in the ground with his tusks, there the rivers ran; and where he struck with his foot, there rose ponds of good water and when he blew through his trunk, – thus, – the trees fell. That was the manner in which the Jungle was made by Tha; and so the tale was told to me.'

'It has not lost fat in the telling,' Bagheera

163

whispered, and Mowgli laughed behind his hand.

'In those days there was no corn or melons or pepper or sugar-cane, nor were there any little huts such as ye have all seen; and the Jungle People knew nothing of Man, but lived in the Jungle together, making one people. But presently they began to dispute over their food, though there was grazing enough for all. They were lazy. Each wished to eat where he lay, as sometimes we can do now when the spring rains are good. Tha, the First of the Elephants, was busy making new jungles and leading the rivers in their beds. He could not walk in all places; therefore he made the First of the Tigers the master and the judge of the Jungle, to whom the Jungle People should bring their disputes. In those days the First of the Tigers ate fruit and grass with the others. He was as large as I am, and he was very beautiful, in colour all over like the blossom of the yellow creeper. There was never stripe nor bar upon his hide in those good days when this the Jungle was new. All the Jungle People came before him without fear, and his word was the Law of all the Jungle. We were then, remember ye, one people.

'Yet upon a night there was a dispute between two bucks – a grazing-quarrel such as ye now settle with the horns and the fore-feet – and it is said that as the two spoke together before the First of the Tigers lying among the flowers, a buck pushed him with his horns, and the First of the Tigers forgot that he was the master and judge of the Jungle, and, leaping upon that buck, broke his neck.

'Till that night never one of us had died, and the First of the Tigers, seeing what he had done, and being made foolish by the scent of the blood, ran away into the marshes of the North, and we of the Jungle, left without a judge, fell to fighting among ourselves; and Tha heard the noise of it and came back. Then some of us said this and some of us said that, but he saw the dead buck among the flowers, and asked who had killed, and we of the Jungle would not tell because the smell of the blood made us foolish. We ran to and fro in circles, capering and crying out and shaking our heads. Then Tha gave an order to the trees that hang low, and to the trailing creepers of the Jungle, that they should mark the killer of the buck so that he should know him again, and he said, "Who will now be master of the Jungle People?" Then up leaped the Gray Ape who lives in the branches, and said, "I will now be master of the Jungle." At this Tha laughed, and said, 'So be it,' and went away very angry.

'Children, ye know the Gray Ape. He was then as he is now. At the first he made a wise face for himself, but in a little while he began to scratch and to leap up and down, and when Tha came back he found the Gray Ape hanging, head down, from a bough, mocking those who stood below; and they mocked him again. And so there was no Law in the Jungle – only foolish talk and senseless words.

'Then Tha called us all together and said: "The first of your masters has brought Death into the Jungle, and the second Shame. Now it is time there was a Law, and a Law that ye must not break. Now ye shall know Fear, and when ye have found him ye shall know that he is your master, and the rest shall follow." Then we of the Jungle said, "What is Fear?" And Tha said, "Seek till ye find." So we went up and down the Jungle seeking for Fear, and presently the buffaloes–'

'Ugh!' said Mysa, the leader of the buffaloes, from their sand-bank.

'Yes, Mysa, it was the buffaloes. They came back with the news that in a cave in the Jungle sat Fear, and that he had no hair, and went upon his hind legs. Then we of the Jungle followed the herd till we came to that cave, and Fear stood at the mouth of it, and he was, as the buffaloes had said, hairless, and he walked upon his hinder legs. When he saw us he cried out, and his voice filled us with the fear that we have now of that voice when we hear it, and we ran away, tramping upon and tearing each other because we were afraid. That night, so it was told to me, we of the Jungle did not lie down together as used to be our custom, but each tribe drew off by itself – the pig with the pig, the deer with the deer; horn to horn, hoof to hoof, – like keeping to like, and so lay shaking in the Jungle.

'Only the First of the Tigers was not with us, for he was still hidden in the marshes of the North, and when word was brought to him of the Thing we had seen in the cave, he said: "I will go to this Thing and break his neck." So he ran all the night till he came to the cave; but the trees and the creepers on his path, remembering the order that Tha had given, let down their branches and marked him as he ran, drawing their fingers across his back, his flank, his forehead, and his jowl. Wherever they touched him there was a mark and a stripe upon his yellow hide. *And those stripes do his children wear to this day!* When he came to the cave, Fear, the Hairless One, put out his hand and called him "The Striped One that comes by night," and the First of the Tigers was afraid of the Hairless One, and ran back to the swamps howling.'

Mowgli chuckled quietly here, his chin in the water.

'So loud did he howl that Tha heard him

and said, "What is the sorrow?" And the First of the Tigers, lifting up his muzzle to the new-made sky, which is now so old, said: "Give me back my power, O Tha. I am made ashamed before all the Jungle, and I have run away from a Hairless One, and he has called me a shameful name." "And why?" said Tha. "Because I am smeared with the mud of the marshes," said the First of the Tigers. "Swim, then, and roll on the wet grass, and if it be mud it will wash away," said Tha; and the First of the Tigers swam, and rolled and rolled upon the grass, till the Jungle ran round and round before his eyes, but not one little bar upon all his hide was changed, and Tha, watching him, laughed. Then the First of the Tigers said, "What have I done that this comes to me?" Tha said, "Thou hast killed the buck, and thou hast let Death loose in the Jungle, and with Death has come Fear, so that the people of the Jungle are afraid one of the other, as thou art afraid of the Hairless One." The First of the Tigers said, "They will never fear me, for I knew them since the beginning." Tha said, "Go and see." And the First of the Tigers ran to and fro, calling aloud to the deer and the pig and the sambhur and the porcupine and all the Jungle Peoples, and they all ran away from him who had been their judge, because they were afraid.

'Then the First of the Tigers came back, and his pride was broken in him, and, beating his head upon the ground, he tore up the earth with all his feet and said: "Remember that I was once the Master of the Jungle. Do not forget me, O Tha! Let my children remember that I was once without shame or fear!" And Tha said: "This much I will do, because thou and I together saw the Jungle made. For one night in each year it shall be as it was before the buck was killed – for thee and for thy children. In that one night, if ye meet the Hairless One – and his name is Man – ye shall not be afraid of him, but he shall be afraid of you, as though ye were judges of the Jungle and masters of all things. Show him mercy in that night of his fear, for thou hast known what Fear is."

'Then the First of the Tigers answered, "I am content"; but when next he drank he saw the black stripes upon his flank and his side, and he remembered the name that the Hairless One had given him, and he was angry. For a year he lived in the marshes, waiting till Tha should keep his promise. And upon a night when the Jackal of the Moon [the Evening Star] stood clear of the Jungle, he felt that his Night was upon him, and he went to that cave to meet the Hairless One. Then it happened as Tha promised, for the Hairless One fell down before him and lay along the ground, and the First of the Tigers struck him and broke his back, for he thought that there was but one such Thing in the Jungle, and that he had killed Fear. Then, nosing above the kill, he heard Tha coming down from the woods of the North, and presently the voice of the First of the Elephants, which is the voice that we hear now–'

The thunder was rolling up and down the dry, scarred hills, but it brought no rain – only heat-lightning that flickered along the ridges – and Hathi went on: *'That* was the voice he heard, and it said: "Is this thy mercy?" The First of the Tigers licked his lips and said: "What matter? I have killed Fear." And Tha said: "O blind and foolish! Thou hast untied the feet of Death, and he will follow thy trail till thou diest. Thou hast taught Man to kill!"

'The First of the Tigers, standing stiffly to his kill, said: "He is as the buck was. There is no Fear. Now I will judge the Jungle Peoples once more."

'And Tha said: "Never again shall the Jungle Peoples come to thee. They shall never cross thy trail, nor sleep near thee, nor follow after thee, nor browse by thy lair. Only Fear shall follow thee, and with a blow that thou canst not see he shall bid thee wait his pleasure. He shall make the ground to open under thy feet, and the creeper to twist about thy neck, and the tree-trunks to grow together about thee higher than thou canst leap, and at the last he shall take thy hide to wrap his cubs when they are cold. Thou hast shown him no mercy, and none will he show thee."

'The First of the Tigers was very bold, for his Night was still on him, and he said: "The Promise of Tha is the Promise of Tha. He will not take away my Night?" And Tha said: "The one Night is thine, as I have said, but there is a price to pay. Thou hast taught Man to kill, and he is no slow learner."

'The First of the Tigers said: "He is here under my foot, and his back is broken. Let the Jungle know I have killed Fear."

'Then Tha laughed, and said: "Thou hast killed one of many, but thou thyself shalt tell the Jungle – for thy Night is ended."

'So the day came; and from the mouth of the cave went out another Hairless One, and he saw the kill in the path, and the First of the Tigers above it, and he took a pointed stick–'

'They throw a thing that cuts now,' said Ikki, rustling down the bank; for Ikki was considered uncommonly good eating by the Gonds – they called him Ho-Igoo – and he knew something of the wicked little Gondee axe that whirls across a clearing like a dragonfly.

'It was a pointed stick, such as they put in the foot of a pit-trap,' said Hathi, 'and

171

throwing it, he struck the First of the Tigers deep in the flank. Thus it happened as Tha said, for the First of the Tigers ran howling up and down the Jungle till he tore out the stick, and all the Jungle knew that the Hairless One could strike from far off, and they feared more than before. So it came about that the First of the Tigers taught the Hairless One to kill – and ye know what harm that has since done to all our peoples – through the noose, and the pitfall, and the hidden trap, and the flying stick, and the stinging fly that comes out of white smoke [Hathi meant the rifle], and the Red Flower that drives us into the open. Yet for one night in the year the Hairless One fears the Tiger, as Tha promised, and never has the Tiger given him cause to be less afraid. Where he finds him, there he kills him, remembering how the First of the Tigers was made ashamed. For the rest, Fear walks up and down the Jungle by day and by night.'

'*Ahi! Aoo!*' said the deer, thinking of what it all meant to them.

'And only when there is one great Fear over all, as there is now, can we of the Jungle lay aside our little fears, and meet together in one place as we do now.'

'For one night only does Man fear the Tiger?' said Mowgli.

'For one night only,' said Hathi.

'But I – but we – but all the Jungle knows that Shere Khan kills Man twice and thrice in a moon.'

'Even so. *Then* he springs from behind and turns his head aside as he strikes, for he is full of fear. If Man looked at him he would run. But on his one Night he goes openly down to the village. He walks between the houses and thrusts his head into the doorway, and the men fall on their faces, and there he does his kill. One kill in that Night.'

'Oh!' said Mowgli to himself, rolling over in the water. '*Now* I see why it was Shere Khan bade me look at him! He got no good of it, for he could not hold his eyes steady, and – and I certainly did not fall down at his feet. But then I am not a man, being of the Free People.'

'Umm!' said Bagheera deep in his furry throat. 'Does the Tiger know his Night?'

'Never till the Jackal of the Moon stands clear of the evening mist. Sometimes it falls in the dry summer and sometimes in the wet rains – this one Night of the Tiger. But for the First of the Tigers, this would never have been, nor would any of us have known fear.'

The deer grunted sorrowfully, and Bagheera's lips curled in a wicked smile. 'Do men know this – tale?' said he.

'None know it except the tigers, and we, the elephants – the children of Tha. Now ye

173

by the pools have heard it, and I have spoken.'

Hathi dipped his trunk into the water as a sign that he did not wish to talk.

'But – but – but,' said Mowgli, turning to Baloo, 'why did not the First of the Tigers continue to eat grass and leaves and trees? He did but break the buck's neck. He did not eat. What led him to the hot meat?'

'The trees and the creepers marked him, Little Brother, and made him the striped thing that we see. Never again would he eat their fruit; but from that day he revenged himself upon the deer, and the others, the Eaters of Grass,' said Baloo.

'Then *thou* knowest the tale. Heh? Why have I never heard?'

'Because the Jungle is full of such tales. If I made a beginning there would never be an end to them. Let go my ear, Little Brother.'

THE LAW OF THE JUNGLE

Just to give you an idea of the immense variety of the Jungle Law, I have translated into verse (Baloo always recited them in a sort of sing-song) a few of the laws that apply to the wolves. There are, of course, hundreds and hundreds more, but these will do for specimens of the simpler rulings.

Now this is the Law of the Jungle – as old and
*   as true as the sky,*
And the Wolf that shall keep it may prosper,
*   but the Wolf that shall break it must die.*

As the creeper that girdles the tree-trunk the
*   Law runneth forward and back –*
For the strength of the Pack is the Wolf, and the
*   strength of the Wolf is the Pack.*

Wash daily from nose-tip to tail-tip; drink
    deeply, but never too deep;
And remember the night is for hunting,
    and forget not the day is for sleep.

The Jackal may follow the Tiger, but, Cub,
    when thy whiskers are grown,
Remember the Wolf is a hunter – go forth

and get food of thine own.

Keep peace with the Lords of the Jungle –
  the Tiger, the Panther, the Bear;
And trouble not Hathi the Silent, and
  mock not the Boar in his lair.

When Pack meets with Pack in the Jungle,
  and neither will go from the trail,
Lie down till the leaders have spoken – it
  may be fair words shall prevail.

When ye fight with a Wolf of the Pack, ye
  must fight him alone and afar,
Lest others take part in the quarrel, and
  the Pack be diminished by war.

The Lair of the Wolf is his refuge, and
  where he has made him his home,
Not even the Head Wolf may enter, not
  even the Council may come.

The Lair of the Wolf is his refuge, but
  where he has digged it too plain,
The Council shall send him a message,
  and so he shall change it again.

If ye kill before midnight, be silent, and
  wake not the woods with your bay,
Lest ye frighten the deer from the crops,
  and the brothers go empty away.

Ye may kill for yourselves, and your mates,
  and your cubs as they need, and ye can;
But kill not for pleasure of killing, and
  seven times never kill Man.

If ye plunder his Kill from a weaker,
  devour not all in thy pride;
Pack-Right is the right of the meanest; so
  leave him the head and the hide.

The Kill of the Pack is the meat of the
  Pack. Ye must eat where it lies;
And no one may carry away of that meat
  to his lair, or he dies.

The Kill of the Wolf is the meat of the
  Wolf. He may do what he will,
But, till he has given permission, the Pack
  may not eat of that Kill.

Cub-Right is the right of the Yearling.
From all of his Pack he may claim
Full-gorge when the killer has eaten; and
  none may refuse him the same.

Lair-Right is the right of the Mother.
From all of her year she may claim
One haunch of each kill for her litter, and
  none may deny her the same.

Cave-Right is the right of the Father – to
  hunt by himself for his own:

177

He is freed of all calls to the Pack; he is
   judged by the Council alone.

Because of his age and his cunning,
   because of his gripe and his paw,
In all that the Law leaveth open, the word
   of the Head Wolf is Law.

*Now these are the Laws of the Jungle, and
   many and mighty are they;*
*But the head and the hoof of the Law and the
   haunch and the hump is – Obey!*

MY LORD THE ELEPHANT

'Less you want your toes trod off you'd
  better get back at once,
For the bullocks are walkin' two by two,
The *byles* are walkin' two by two,
The bullocks are walkin' two by two,
An' the elephants bring the guns!
Ho! Yuss!
Great – big – long – black forty-pounder
  guns:
Jiggery-jolty to and fro,
Each as big as a launch in tow –
Blind – dumb – broad-breeched beggars
  o' batterin' guns!

               Barrack-Room Ballad.

Touching the truth of this tale there need be
no doubt at all, for it was told to me by
Mulvaney at the back of the elephant-lines,
one warm evening when we were taking the
dogs out for exercise. The twelve Government elephants rocked at their pickets
outside the big mud-walled stables (one
arch, as wide as a bridge-arch, to each
restless beast), and the mahouts were
preparing the evening meal. Now and again
some impatient youngster would smell the

cooking flour-cakes and squeal; and the naked little children of the elephant-lines would strut down the row shouting and commanding silence, or, reaching up, would slap at the eager trunks. Then the elephants feigned to be deeply interested in pouring dust upon their heads, but, so soon as the children passed, the rocking, fidgeting, and muttering broke out again.

The sunset was dying, and the elephants heaved and swayed dead black against the one sheet of rose-red low down in the dusty grey sky. It was at the beginning of the hot weather, just after the troops had changed into their white clothes, so Mulvaney and Ortheris looked like ghosts walking through the dusk. Learoyd had gone off to another barrack to buy sulphur ointment for his last dog under suspicion of mange, and with delicacy had put his kennel into quarantine at the back of the furnace where they cremate the anthrax cases.

'*You* wouldn't like mange, little woman?' said Ortheris, turning my terrier over on her fat white back with his foot. 'You're no end bloomin' partic'lar, you are. 'Oo wouldn't take no notice o' me t'other day 'cause she was goin' 'ome all alone in 'er dorg-cart, eh? Settin' on the box-seat like a bloomin' little tart, you was, Vicky. Now you run along an' make them 'uttees' 'oller. Sick 'em, Vicky, loo!'

Elephants loathe little dogs. Vixen barked herself down the pickets, and in a minute all the elephants were kicking and squealing and clucking together.

'Oh, you soldier-men,' said a mahout angrily, 'call off your she-dog. She is frightening our elephant-folk.'

'Rummy beggars!' said Ortheris meditatively. 'Call 'em people, same as if they was. An' they are too. Not so bloomin' rummy when you come to think of it, neither.'

Vixen returned yapping to show that she could do it again if she liked, and established herself between Ortheris's knees, smiling a large smile at his lawful dogs who dared not fly at her.

'Seed the battery this mornin'?' said Ortheris. He meant the newly-arrived elephant-battery; otherwise he would have said simply 'guns.' Three elephants harnessed tandem go to each gun, and those who have not seen the big forty-pounders of position trundling along in the wake of their gigantic team have yet something to behold. The lead-elephant had behaved very badly on parade; had been cut loose, sent back to the lines in disgrace, and was at that hour squealing and lashing out with his trunk at the end of the line; a picture of blind, bound, bad temper. His mahout, standing clear of the flail-like blows, was trying to soothe him.

181

'That's the beggar that cut up on p'rade. 'E's *must*,' said Ortheris pointing. 'There'll be murder in the lines soon, and then, per'aps, 'e'll get loose an' we'll 'ave to be turned out to shoot 'im, same as when one o' they native kings' elephants *musted* last June. 'Ope 'e will.'

'*Must* be sugared!' said Mulvaney contemptuously from his resting-place on the pile of dried bedding. 'He's no more than in a powerful bad timper wid bein' put upon. I'd lay my kit he's new to the gun-team, an' by natur' he hates haulin'. Ask the mahout, sorr.'

I hailed the old white-bearded mahout who was lavishing pet words on his sulky red-eyed charge.

'He is not *musth*,' the man replied indignantly; 'only his honour has been touched. Is an elephant an ox or a mule that he should tug at a trace? His strength is in his head – Peace, peace, my Lord! It was not *my* fault that they yoked thee this morning! – Only a low-caste elephant will pull a gun, and *he* is a Kumeria of the Doon. It cost a year and the life of a man to break him to burden. They of the Artillery put him in the gunteam because one of their base-born brutes had gone lame. No wonder that he was and is wrath.'

'Rummy! Most unusual rum,' said Ortheris. 'Gawd, 'e is in a temper, though!

182

S'pose 'e got loose!'

Mulvaney began to speak but checked himself, and I asked the mahout what would happen if the heel-chains broke.

'God knows, Who made elephants,' he said simply. 'In his now state peradventure he might kill you three, or run at large till his rage abated. He would not kill me except he were *musth*. *Then* would he kill me before anyone in the world, because he loves me. Such is the custom of the elephant-folk; and the custom of us mahout-people matches it for foolishness. We trust each our own elephant, till our own elephant kills us. Other castes trust women, but we the elephant-folk. I have seen men deal with enraged elephants and live; but never was man yet born of woman that met my lord the elephant in his *musth* and lived to tell of the taming. They are enough bold who meet him angry.'

I translated. Then said Terence: 'Ask the heathen if he iver saw a man tame an elephint, – anyways – a white man.'

'Once,' said the mahout, 'I saw a man astride of such a beast in the town of Cawnpore; a bare-headed man, a white man, beating it upon the head with a gun. It was said he was possessed of devils or drunk.'

'Is ut like, think you, he'd be doin' ut sober?' said Mulvaney after interpretation, and the chained elephant roared.

'There's only one man top of earth that would be the partic'lar kind o' sorter bloomin' fool to do it!' said Ortheris. 'When was that, Mulvaney?'

'As the naygur sez, in Cawnpore; an' I was that fool – in the days av my youth. But ut came about as naturil as wan thing leads to another, – me an' the elephint, an' the elephint an' me; an' the fight betune us was the most naturil av all.'

'That's just wot it would ha' been,' said Ortheris. 'Only you must ha' been more than usual full. You done one queer trick with an elephant that I know of, why didn't you never tell us the other one?'

'Bekase, onless you had heard the naygur here say what he has said spontaneous, you'd ha' called me for a liar, Stanley, my son, an' it would ha' bin my juty an' my delight to give you the father an' mother av a beltin'! There's only wan fault about you, little man, an' that's thinking you know all there is in the world, an' a little more. 'Tis a fault that has made away wid a few orf'cers I've served undher, not to spake av ivry man but two that I iver thried to make into a privit.'

'Ho!' said Ortheris with ruffled plumes, 'an' oo was your two bloomin' little Sir Garnets, eh?'

'Wan was mesilf,' said Mulvaney with a

184

grin that darkness could not hide; 'an' – seem' that he's not here there's no harm speakin' av him – t'other was Jock.'

'Jock's no more than a 'ayrick in trousies. 'E be'aves *like* one; an 'e can't 'it one at a undred; 'e was born *on* one, an s'welp me 'e'll die *under* one for not bein' able to say wot 'e wants in a Christian lingo,' said Ortheris, jumping up from the piled fodder only to be swept off his legs. Vixen leaped upon his stomach, and the other dogs followed and sat down there.

'I know what Jock is like,' I said. 'I want to hear about the elephant, though.'

'It's another o' Mulvaney's bloomin' panoramas,' said Ortheris, gasping under the dogs. ''Im an' Jock for the 'ole bloomin' British Army! You'll be sayin' you won Waterloo next, – you an' Jock. Garn!'

Neither of us thought it worth while to notice Ortheris. The big gun-elephant threshed and muttered in his chains, giving tongue now and again in crashing trumpet-peals, and to this accompaniment Terence went on: 'In the beginnin',' said he, 'me bein' what I was, there was a misundherstandin' wid my sargint that was then. He put his spite on me for various reasons'–

The deep-set eyes twinkled above the glow of the pipe-bowl, and Ortheris grunted, 'Another petticoat!'

–'For various an' promiscuous reasons;

an' the upshot av it was that he come into barricks wan afternoon whin I was settlin' my cowlick before goin' walkin', called me a big baboon (which I was not), an' a demoralisin' beggar (which I was), an' bid me go on fatigue thin an' there, helpin' shift EP tents, fourteen av thim from the rest-camps. At that, me bein' set on my walk–'

'Ah!' from under the dogs, ''e's a Mormon, Vic. Don't you 'ave nothin' to do with 'im, little dorg.'

–'Set on my walk, I tould him a few things that came up in my mind, an' wan thing led on to another, an' betune talkin' I made time for to hit the nose av him so that he'd be no Venus to any woman for a week to come. 'Twas a fine big nose, and well it paid for a little groomin'. Afther that I was so well pleased wid my handicraftfulness that I niver raised fist on the gyard that came to take me to Clink. A child might ha' led me along, for I knew old Kearney's nose was ruined. That summer the Ould Rig'mint did not use their own Clink, bekase the cholera was hangin' about there like mildew on wet boots, an' 'twas murdher to confine in ut. We borrowed the Clink that belonged to the Holy Christians (the rig'mint that has never seen service yet), and that lay a matther av a mile away, acrost two p'rade-grounds an' the main road, an' all the ladies av Cawnpore goin' out for their afternoon dhrive. So

I moved in the best av society, my shadow dancin' along forninst me, an the gyard as solemn as putty, the bracelets on my wrists, an' my heart full contint wid the notion av Kearney's pro-proprobosculum in a shling.

'In the middle av ut all I perceived a gunner-orf'cer in full rig'mintals perusin' down the road, hell-for-leather, wid his mouth open. He fetched wan woild despairin' look on the dog-kyarts an' the polite society av Cawnpore, an' thin he dived like a rabbut into a dhrain by the side av the road.

'"Bhoys," sez I, "that orf'cer's dhrunk. 'Tis scand'lus. Let's take him to Clink too."

'The corp'ril of the gyard made a jump for me, unlocked my stringers, an' he sez: "If it comes to runnin', run for your life. If it doesn't, I'll trust your honour. Anyways," sez he, "come to Clink whin you can."

'Then I behild him runnin' wan way, stuffin' the bracelets in his pocket, they bein' Gov'ment property, an' the gyard runnin' another, an' all the dog-kyarts runnin' all ways to wanst, an' me alone lookin' down the red bag av a mouth av an elephint forty-two feet high at the shoulder, tin feet wide, wid tusks as long as the Ochterlony Monumint. That was my first reconnaissance. Maybe he was not quite so contagious, nor quite so tall, but I didn't stop to throw out pickuts. Mother av Hiven, how I ran down the road! The baste began to inveshtigate the dhrain wid the gunner-orf'cer in ut; an' that was the makin' av me. I tripped over wan of the rifles that my gyard had discarded (onsoldierly blackguards they was!), and whin I got up I was facin' t'other way about an' the elephint was huntin' for the gunner-orf'cer. I can see his big fat back yet. Excipt that he didn't dig, he carried on for all the world like little Vixen here at a rat-hole. He put his head down (by my sowl, he nearly stud on ut!) to shquint down the dhrain; thin he'd grunt, and run round to the other ind in case the orf'cer was gone out by the back door; an' he'd shtuff his trunk down the flue an' get ut filled wid mud, an' blow ut out, an' grunt, an' swear! My troth, he swore all hiven down upon that orf'cer; an' what a commissariat elephint had to do wid a gunner-orf'cer passed me. Me havin' nowhere to go excipt to Clink, I stud in the road wid the rifle, a Snider an' no amm'nition, philosophisin' upon the rear ind av the animal. All round me, miles an' miles, there was howlin' desolation, for ivry human sowl wid two legs, or four for the matther av that, was ambuscadin', an' this ould rapparee stud on his head tuggin' an' gruntin' above the dhrain, his tail stickin' up to the sky, an' he thryin' to thrumpet through three feet av road-sweepin's up his thrunk. Begad, 'twas wickud to behold!

'Subsequint he caught sight av me standin' alone in the wide, wide world lanin' on the rifle. That dishcomposed him, bekase he thought I was the gunner-orf'cer got out unbeknownst. He looked betune his feet at the dhrain, an' he looked at me, an' I sez to mesilf: 'Terence, my son, you've been watchin' this Noah's ark too long. Run for your life!' Dear knows I wanted to tell him I was only a poor privit on my way to Clink, an' no orf'cer at all, at all; but he put his ears forward av his thick head, an' I rethreated down the road grippin' the rifle, my back as cowld as a tombstone, an' the slack av my trousies, where I made sure he'd take hoult, crawlin' wid – wid invidjus apprehension.

'I might ha' run till I dhropped, bekase I was betune the two straight lines av the road, an' a man, or a thousand men for the matther av that, are the like av sheep in keepin' betune right an' left marks.'

'Same as canaries,' said Ortheris from the darkness. 'Draw a line on a bloomin' little board, put their bloomin' little beakses there; stay so for hever and hever, amen, they will. 'Seed a 'ole reg'ment, I 'ave, walk crabways along the edge of a two-foot water-cut 'stid o' thinkin' to cross it. Men is sheep – bloomin' sheep. Go on.'

'But I saw his shadow wid the tail av my eye,' continued the man of experiences, 'an' "Wheel," I sez, "Terence, wheel!" an' I wheeled. 'Tis truth I cud hear the shparks flyin' from my heels; an' I shpun into the nearest compound, fetched wan jump from the gate to the veranda av the house, an' fell over a tribe of naygurs wid a half-caste boy at a desk, all manufacturin' harness. 'Twas Antonio's Carriage Emporium at Cawnpore. You know ut, sorr?

'Ould Grambags must ha' wheeled abreast wid me, for his trunk came lickin' into the veranda like a belt in a barrick-room row, before I was in the shop. The naygurs an' the half-caste boy howled an' wint out at the back door, an' I stud lone as Lot's wife among the harness. A powerful thirsty thing is harness, by reason av the smell to ut.

'I wint into the back room, nobody bein' there to invite, an' I found a bottle av whisky and a goglet av wather. The first an' the second dhrink I never noticed, bein' dhry, but the fourth an' the fifth tuk good hoult av me an' I began to think scornful av elephints. 'Take the upper ground in manoe'vrin', Terence,' I sez; 'an' you'll be a gin'ral yet,' sez I. An' wid that I wint up to the flat mud roof av the house an' looked over the edge av the parapit, threadin' delicate. Ould Barrel-belly was in the compound, walkin' to an' fro, pluckin' a piece av grass here an' a weed there, for all the world like our Colonel that is now whin his wife's given him a talkin'-down an' he's prom'nadin' to ease his timper. His back was to me, an by the same token I hiccupped. He checked in his walk, wan ear forward like a deaf ould lady wid an ear-thrumpet, an' his thrunk hild out in a kind av fore-reaching hook. Thin he wagged his ear sayin', 'Do my sinses deceive me?' as plain as print, an' he recomminst prom-enadin'. You know Antonio's compound? 'Twas as full thin as 'tis now av new kyarts an' ould kyarts, an' second-hand kyarts an' kyarts for hire – landos, an' b'rooshes an' brooms, an wag'nettes av ivry description. Thin I hiccupped again, an' he began to study the ground beneath him, his tail whistlin' wid emotion. Thin he lapped his thrunk round the shaft av a wag'nette an' dhrew it out circumspectuous an' thought-ful. 'He's not there,' he sez, fumblin' in the cushions wid his thrunk. Thin I hiccupped again, an' wid that he lost his patience good an' all, same as this wan in the lines here.'

The gun-elephant was breaking into peal after peal of indignant trumpetings, to the disgust of the other animals who had finished their food and wished to drowse. Between the outcries we could hear him picking restlessly at his ankle-ring.

'As I was sayin',' Mulvaney went on, 'he behaved dishgraceful. He let out wid his fore-fut like a steam-hammer, bein' con-vinced that I was in ambuscade adjacent; an' that wag'nette ran back among the other carriages like a field-gun in charge. Thin he hauled ut out again an' shuk ut, an' by natur' ut came all to little pieces. Afther that he went sheer damn, slam, dancin', lunatic, double-shuffle demented wid the whole of Antonio's shtock for the season. He kicked, an' he straddled, an' he stamped, an' he pounded all at wanst, his big bald head bobbin' up an' down, solemn as a rigadoon. He tuk a new shiny broom an' kicked ut on wan corner, an ut opened out like a blossomin' lily; an' he shtuck wan fool-fut through the flure av ut an' a wheel was shpinnin' on his tusk. At that he got scared, an' by this an' that he fair sat down plump among the carriages, an' they pricked him wid splinters till he was a boundin' pincushin. In the middle av the mess, whin the kyarts was climbin' wan on top av the other, an' rickochettin' off the mud walls, an' showin' their agility, wid him tearin' their wheels off, I heard the sound av distrestful wailin' on the housetops, an the whole Antonio firm an' fam'ly was cursin' me an' him from the roof next door; me bekase I'd taken refuge wid them, and he bekase he was playin' shtep-dances wid the carriages av the aristocracy.

'"Divart his attention," sez Antonio, dancin on the roof in his big white waistcoat. "Divart his attention," he sez, "or I'll prosecute you." An' the whole fam'ly shouts, "Hit him a kick, mister soldier."

'"He's divartin' himself," I sez, for it was just the worth av a man's life to go down into the compound. But by way av makin' show I threw the whisky-bottle ('twas not full whin I came there) at him. He sphun round from fwhat was left av the last kyart, an' shtuck his head into the veranda not three feet below me. Maybe 'twas the temptin'ness av his back or the whisky. Anyways, the next thing I knew was me, wid my hands full av mud an' mortar, all fours on his back, an' the Snider just slidin' off the slope av his head. I grabbed that an' scuffled on his neck, dhruv my knees undher his big flappin' ears, an we wint to glory out av that compound wid a shqueal that crawled up my back an' down my belly. Thin I remimbered the Snider, an' I grup ut by the muzzle an' hit him on the head. 'Twas most forlorn – like tappin' the deck av a throopship wid a cane to stop the engines whin you're sea-sick. But I parsevered till I sweated, an' at last from takin' no notice at all he began to grunt. I hit wid the full strength that was in me in those days, an' it might ha' discommoded him. We came back to the p'rade-groun' forty miles an hour, trumpetin' vainglorious. I niver stopped hammerin' him for a minut'; 'twas by way av divartin' him from runnin' undher the trees an' scrapin' me off like a poultice. The p'rade-groun' an' the road was all empty, but the throops was on the roofs av the barricks, an' betune Ould Thrajectory's gruntin' an mine (for I was winded wid my stone-breakin'), I heard thim clappin' an' cheerin'. He was growin' more confused an' tuk to runnin in circles.

'Begad,' sez I to mesilf, 'there's dacincy in all things, Terence. 'Tis like you've shplit his head, and whin you come out av Clink you'll be put undher stoppages for killin' a Gov'mint elephint.' At that I caressed him.'

''Ow the devil did you do that? Might as well pat a barrick,' said Ortheris.

'Thried all manner av endearin' epitaphs, but bein' more than a little shuk up I disremimbered what the divil would answer to. So, "Good dog," I sez; "Pretty puss," sez I; "Whoa mare," I sez; an' at that I fetched him a shtroke av the butt for to conciliate him, an' he stud still among the barricks.

'"Will no one take me off the top av this murderin' volcano?" I sez at the top av my shout; an' I heard a man yellin', "Hould on, faith an' patience, the other elephints are comin'." "Mother av Glory," I sez, "will I rough-ride the whole stud? Come an' take me down, ye cowards!"

'Thin a brace av fat she-elephints wid mahouts an a commissariat sargint came shufflin' round the corner av the barricks an' the mahouts was abusin' ould Potiphar's

194

mother an' blood-kin.

'"Obsarve my reinforcements," I sez. "They're goin' to take you to Clink, my son"; an' the child av calamity put his ears forward an swung head on to those females. The pluck av him, afther my oratorio on his brain-pan, wint to the heart av me. "I'm in dishgrace mesilf," I sez, "but I'll do what I can for ye. Will ye go to Clink like a man, or fight like a fool whin there's no chanst?" Wid that I fetched him wan last lick on the head, an' he fetched a tremenjus groan an' dhropped his thrunk. "Think," sez I to him, an' "Halt!" I sez to the mahouts. They was anxious so to do. I could feel the ould reprobit meditatin' undher me. At last he put his thrunk straight out an' gave a most melancholious toot (the like av a sigh wid an elephint); an' by that I knew the white flag was up an' the rest was no more than considherin' his feelin's.

'"He's done," I sez. "Kape open ordher left an' right alongside. We'll go to Clink quiet."

'Sez the commissariat sargint to me from his elephint, "Are you a man or a mericle?" sez he.

'"I'm betwixt an' betune," I sez, thryin' to set up stiff-back. "An' fwhat," sez I, "may ha' set this animal off in this opprobrious shtyle?" I sez, the gun-butt light an' easy on my hip an' my left hand dhropped, such as

195

throopers behave. We was bowlin' on to the elephint-lines undher escort all this time.

"'I was not in the lines whin the throuble began," sez the sargint. "They tuk him off carryin' tents an' such like, an' put him to the gun-team. I knew he would not like ut, but by token ut fair tore his heart out."

"'Faith, wan man's meat is another's poison," I sez. "'Twas bein' put on to carry tents that was the ruin av me." An' my heart warrumed to Ould Double Ends bekase he had been put upon.

"'We'll close on him here," sez the sargint, whin we got to the elephint-lines. All the mahouts an' their childher was round the pickuts cursin' my pony from a mile to hear. "You skip off on to my elephint's back," he sez. "There'll be throuble."

"'Sind that howlin' crowd away," I sez, "or he'll thrample the life out av thim." I cud feel his ears beginnin' to twitch. "An' do you an' your immoril she-elephints go well clear away. I will get down here. He's an Irishman," I sez, "for all his long Jew's nose, an' he shall be threated like an Irishman."

"'Are ye tired av life?" sez the sargint.

"'Divil a bit," I sez; "but wan av us has to win, an' I'm av opinion 'tis me. Get back," I sez.

'The two elephints wint off, an' Smith O'Brine came to a halt dead above his own pickuts. "Down," sez I, whackin' him on the head, an' down he wint, shouldher over shouldher like a hill-side slippin' afther rain. "Now," sez I, slidin' down his nose an' runnin, to the front av him, "you will see the man that's betther than you."

'His big head was down betune his big forefeet, an' they was twisted in sideways like a kitten's. He looked the picture av innocince an' forlornsomeness, an' by this an' that his big hairy undherlip was thremblin', an' he winked his eyes together to kape from cryin'. "For the love av God," I sez, clean forgettin' he was a dumb baste, "don't take ut to heart so! Aisy, be aisy," I sez; an' wid that I rubbed his cheek an' betune his eyes an' the top av his thrunk, talkin' all the time. "Now," sez I, "I'll make you comfortable for the night. Send wan or two childher here," I sez to the sargint who was watchin' for to see me killed. "He'll rouse at the sight av a man."'

'You got bloomin' clever all of a sudden,' said Ortheris. ''Ow did you come to know 'is funny little ways that soon?'

'Bekase,' said Terence with emphasis, 'bekase I had conquered the beggar, my son.'

'Ho!' said Ortheris between doubt and derision. 'G'on.'

'His mahout's child an' wan or two other line-babies came runnin' up, not bein' afraid av anything, an' some got wather, an'

197

I washed the top av his poor sore head (begad, I had done him to a turn!), an' some picked the pieces av carts out av his hide, an' we scraped him, an' handled him all over, an' we put a thunderin' big poultice av neem-leaves (the same that we stick on a pony's gall) on his head, an' it looked like a smokin'-cap, an' we put a pile av young sugar-cane forninst him, an' he began to pick at ut. "Now," sez I, settin' down on his fore-fut, "we'll have a dhrink, an' let bygones be." I sent a naygur-child for a quart av arrack, an' the sargint's wife she sint me out four fingers av whisky, an' when the liquor came I cud see by the twinkle in Ould Typhoon's eye that he was no more a stranger to ut me! So he tuk his quart like a Christian, an' *thin* I put his shackles on than me, – worse luck, than, chained him fore an' aft to the pickuts, an' gave him my blessin' an' wint back to barricks.'

'And after?' I said in the pause.

'Ye can guess,' said Mulvaney. 'There was confusion, an' the Colonel gave me ten rupees, an' the Adj'tant gave me five, an my Comp'ny Captain gave me five, an' the men carried me round the barricks shoutin'.'

'Did you go to Clink?' said Ortheris.

'I niver heard a word more about the misundherstandin' wid Kearney's beak, if that's what you mane; but sev'ril av the bhoys was tuk off sudden to the Holy

Christians' Hotel that night. Small blame to thim, – they had twenty rupees in dhrinks. I wint to lie down an' sleep ut off, for I was as done an' double-done as him there in the lines. 'Tis no small thing to go ride elephints.

'Subsequint, me an' the Venerable Father av Sin became mighty frindly. I wud go down to the lines, whin I was in dishgrace, an' spend an afthernoon collogin' wid him; he chewin' wan stick av sugar-cane an' me another, as thick as thieves. He'd take all I had out av my pockets an' put ut back again, an' now an' thin I'd bring him beer for his dijistin, an' I'd give him advice about bein' well behaved an' keepin' off the books. Afther that he wint the way av the Army, an' that's bein' thransferred as soon as you've made a good frind.'

'So you never saw him again?' I demanded.

'Do you belave the first half av the affair?' said Terence.

'I'll wait till Learoyd comes,' I said evasively. Except when he was carefully tutored by the other two and the immediate money-benefit explained, the Yorkshireman did not tell lies; and Terence, I knew, had a profligate imagination.

'There's another part still,' said Mulvaney. 'Ortheris was in that.'

'Then I'll believe it all,' I answered, not from any special belief in Ortheris's word, but from desire to learn the rest. Ortheris stole a pup from me when our acquaintance was new, and, with the little beast stifling under his overcoat, denied not only the theft, but that he ever was interested in dogs.

'That was at the beginnin' av the Afghan business,' said Mulvaney; 'years afther the men that had seen me do the thrick was dead or gone Home. I came not to speak av ut at the last, – bekase I do *not* care to knock the face av ivry man that calls me a liar. At the very beginnin' av the marchin' I wint sick like a fool. I had a boot-gall, but I was all for keepin' up wid the Rig'mint and such like foolishness. So I finished up wid a hole in my heel that you cud ha' dhruv a tent-peg into. Faith, how often have I preached that to recruities since, for a warnin' to thim to look afther their feet! Our docthor, who knew our business as well as his own, he sez to me, in the middle av the Tangi Pass it was: "That's sheer damned carelessness," sez he. "How often have I tould you that a marchin' man is no stronger than his feet, – his feet, – his feet!" he sez. "Now to hospital you go," he sez, "for three weeks, an expense to your Quane an' a nuisince to your counthry. Next time," sez he, "perhaps you'll put some av the whisky you pour down your throat, an some av the tallow you put into your hair, into your socks," sez he. Faith, he was a just man. So soon as we come to the head av the Tangi I wint to hospital, hoppin' on wan fut, woild wid disappointmint. 'Twas a field-hospital (all flies an' native apothecaries an' liniment) dhropped, in a way av speakin', close by the head av the Tangi. The hospital gyard was ravin' mad wid us sick for kapin' thim there, an' we was ravin' mad at bein' kept; an' through the Tangi, day an' night an' night an' day, the fut an' horse an' guns an' commissariat an' tents an' followers av the brigades was pourin' like a coffee-mill. The doolies came dancin' through, scores an scores av thim, an' they'd turn up the hill to hospital wid their sick, an' I lay in bed nursin' my heel, an' hearin' the men bein' tuk out. I remimber wan night (the time I was tuk wid fever) a man came rowlin' through the tents an', "Is there any room to die here?" he sez; "there's none wid the columns"; an' at that he dhropped dead acrost a cot, an thin the man in ut began to complain against dyin' all alone in the dust undher dead men. Thin I must ha' turned mad wid the fever, an' for a week I was prayin' the saints to stop the noise av the columns movin' through the Tangi. Gunwheels it was that wore my head thin. Ye know how 'tis wid fever?'

We nodded; there was no need to explain.

'Gun-wheels an' feet an' people shoutin', but mostly gunwheels. 'Twas neither night

nor day to me for a week. In the mornin'
they'd rowl up the tent-flies, an' we sick cud
look at the Pass an' considher what was
comin' next. Horse, fut, or guns, they'd be
sure to dhrop wan or two sick wid us an'
we'd get news. Wan mornin', whin the fever
hild off av me, I was watchin' the Tangi, an'
'twas just like the picture on the backside av
the Afghan medal – men an' elephints an'
guns comin' wan at a time crawlin' out av a
dhrain.'

'It *were* a drain,' said Ortheris with feeling.
'I've fell out an' been sick in the Tangi twice;
an' wot turns my innards ain't no bloomin'
vi'lets neither.'

'The Pass gave a twist at the ind, so
everything shot out suddint an' they'd built
a throop-bridge (mud an' dead mules) over
a nullah at the had av ut. I lay an' counted
the elephints (gun-elephints) thryin' the
bridge wid their thrunks an' rollin' out
sagacious. The fifth elephint's head came
round the corner, an' he threw up his
thrunk, an' he fetched a toot, an' there he
shtuck at the head of the Tangi like a cork in
a bottle. "Faith," thinks I to mesuf, "he will
not thrust the bridge; there will be
throuble."

'Trouble! My Gawd!' said Ortheris.
'Terence, *I* was be'ind that blooming 'uttee
up to my stock in dust. Trouble!'

'Tell on, then, little man; I only saw the

202

hospital ind av ut.' Mulvaney knocked the ashes out of his pipe, as Ortheris heaved the dogs aside and went on.

'We was escort to them guns, three comp'nies of us,' he said. 'Dewcy was our Major, an our orders was to roll up anything we come across in the Tangi an' shove it out t'other end. Sort o' pop-gun picnic, see? We'd rolled up a lot o' lazy beggars o' native followers, an' some commissariat supplies that was bivoo-whackin' for ever seemin'ly, an' all the sweepin's of 'arf a dozen things what ought to 'ave bin at the front weeks ago, an Dewcy, he sez to us: "You're most 'eart-breakin' sweeps," 'e sez. "For 'eving's sake,' sez 'e, 'do a little sweepin' now." So we swep', – s'welp me, 'ow we did sweep 'em along! There was a full reg'ment be'ind us; most anxious to get on they was; an' they kep' on sendin' to us with the Colonel's compliments, an' what in 'ell was we stoppin' the way for, please? Oh, they was partic'lar polite! So was Dewcy! 'E sent 'em back wot-for, an' 'e give us wot-for, an' we give the guns wot-for, an' they give the the commissariat wot-for, an' the Commissariat give first-class extry wot-for to the native followers, an on we'd go again till we was stuck, an' the 'ole Pass 'ud be swimmin'-Allelujah for a mile an' a 'arf. We 'adn't no tempers, nor no seats to our trousies, an' our coats an our rifles was chucked in the carts, so as we might ha' been cut up any minute, an' we was doin' drover-work. That was wot it was; drovin' on the Islin'ton road!

'I was close up at the 'ead of the column when we saw the end of the Tangi openin' out ahead of us, an' I sez: "The door's open, boys. 'Oo'll git to the gall'ry fust?" I sez. Then I saw Dewcy screwin' 'is bloomin' eyeglass in 'is eye an' lookin' straight on. "Propped, – *ther* beggar!" he sez; an' the be'ind end o' that bloomin' old 'uttee was shinin' through the dust like a bloomin' old moon made o' tarpaulin. Then we 'alted, all chock-a-block, one atop o' the other, an' right at the back o' the guns there sails in a lot o' silly grinnin' camels, wot the commissariat was in charge of – sailin' away as if they was at the Zoological Gardens an' squeezin' our men most awful. The dust was that up you couldn't see your 'and; an' the more we 'it 'em on the 'ead the more their drivers sez, "Accha! Accha!" an' by Gawd it was "at yer" before you knew where you was. An' that 'uttee's be'ind end stuck in the Pass good an' tight, an' no one knew wot for.

'Fust thing we 'ad to do was to fight them bloomin' camels. I wasn't goin' to be eat by no bull-*oont*; so I 'eld up my trousies with one 'and, standin' on a rock, an' 'it away with my belt at every nose I saw bobbin' above me. Then the camels fell back, an'

204

they 'ad to fight to keep the rearguard an' the native followers from crushin' into them; an' the rear-guard 'ad to send down the Tangi to warn the other reg'ment that we was blocked. I 'eard the mahouts shoutin' in front that the 'uttee wouldn't cross the bridge; an' I saw Dewcy skippin' about through the dust like a musquito-worm in a tank. Then our comp'nies got tired o' waitin' an' begun to mark time, an' some goat struck up *Tommy, make room for your Uncle*. After *that*, you couldn't neither see nor breathe nor 'ear; an' there we was singin' bloomin' serenades to the end of a' elephant that don't care for tunes! I sung too; I couldn't do nothin' else. They was strengthenin' the bridge in front, all for the sake of the 'uttee. By an' by a' orf'cer caught me by the throat an' choked the sing out of me. So I caught the next man I could see by the throat an' choked the sing out of 'im.'

'What's the difference between being choked by an officer and being hit?' I asked, remembering a little affair in which Ortheris's honour had been injured by his lieutenant.

'One's a bloomin' lark, an' one's a bloomin' insult!' said Ortheris. 'Besides, we was on service, an' no one cares what an orf'cer does then, s'long as 'e gets our rations an' don't get us unusual cut up. After that we got quiet, an' I 'eard Dewcy say that 'e'd court-martial the lot of us soon as we was out of the Tangi. Then we give three cheers for Dewcy an' three more for the Tangi; an' the 'uttee's be'ind end was stickin' in the Pass, so we cheered *that*. Then they said the bridge had been strengthened, an' we give three cheers for the bridge; but the 'uttee wouldn't move a bloomin' hinch. Not 'im! Then we cheered 'im again, an' Kite Dawson, that was corner-man at all the sing-songs ('e died on the way down), began to give a nigger lecture on the be'ind ends of elephants, an' Dewcy, 'e tried to keep 'is face for a minute, but, Lord, you couldn't do such when Kite was playin' the fool an' askin' whether 'e mightn't 'ave leave to rent a villa an' raise is orphan children in the Tangi, cos 'e couldn't get 'ome no more. Then up come a' orf'cer (mounted, like a fool, too) from the reg'ment at the back with some more of his Colonel's pretty little compliments, an' what was this delay, please? We sung 'im *There's another bloomin' row downstairs* till 'is 'orse bolted, an' then we give 'im three cheers; an' Kite Dawson sez 'e was goin' to write to *The Times* about the awful state of the streets in Afghanistan. The 'uttee's be'ind end was stickin' in the Pass all the time. At last one o' the mahouts came to Dewcy an' sez something. "Oh Lord!" sez Dewcy, *"I don't know the beggar's visiting-list! I'll give 'im another ten minutes an' then*

I'll shoot 'im." Things was gettin' pretty dusty in the Tangi, so we all listened. 'E wants to see a friend,' sez Dewcy out loud to the men, an' 'e mopped 'is forehead an' sat down on a gun-tail.

'I leave it to you to judge 'ow the Reg'ment shouted. "That's all right," we sez. "Three cheers for Mister Winter-bottom's friend," sez we. "Why didn't you say so at first? Pass the word for old Swizzletail's wife," – and such like. Some o' the men they didn't laugh. They took it same as if it might have been a' introduction like, 'cos they knew about 'uttees. Then we all run forward over the guns an in an' out among the elephants' legs – Lord, I wonder 'arf the comp'nies wasn't squashed – an' the next thing I saw was Terence 'ere, lookin' like a sheet o' wet paper, comin' down the 'illside wid a sergeant. "Strewth," I sez, "I might ha' knowed 'e'd be at the bottom of any cat's trick," sez I. Now you tell wot 'appened your end?'

'I lay be the same as you did, little man, listenin' to the noises an' the bhoys singin'. Presintly I heard whisperin' an' the docthor sayin', "Get out av this, wakin' my sick wid your jokes about elephints." An' another man sez, all angry: "'Tis a joke that is stoppin' two thousand men in the Tangi. That son av sin av a haybag av an elephint sez, or the mahouts sez for him, that he wants to see a frind, an' he'll not lift hand or fut till he finds him. I'm wore out wid inthrojucin' sweepers an' coolies to him, an' his hide's as full o' baynit pricks as a musquito-net av holes, an' I'm here undher ordhers, docthor dear, to ask if anyone, sick or well, or alive or dead, knows an elephint. I'm not mad," he sez, settin' on a box av medical comforts. "'Tis my ordhers, an' 'tis my mother," he sez, "that would laugh at me for the father av all fools today. Does any wan here know an elephint?" We sick was all quiet.

"'Now you've had your answer,' sez the docthor. "Go away."

"'Hould on," I sez, thinkin' mistiways in my cot, an' I did not know my own voice. "I'm by way av bein' acquainted wid an elephint, myself," I sez.

"'That's delirium," sez the docthor. "See what you've done, sargint. Lie down, man," he sez, seem' me thryin' to get up.

"''Tis not," I sez. "I rode him round Cawnpore barricks. He will not ha' forgotten. I bruk his head wid a rifle."

"'Mad as a coot," sez the docthor, an' thin he felt my head. "It's quare," sez he. "Man," he sez, "if you go, d'you know 'twill either kill or cure?"

"'What do I care?" sez I. "If I'm mad, 'tis better dead."

"'Faith, that's sound enough," sez the

docthor. "You've no fever on you now."

"'Come on,' sez the sargint. "We're all mad to-day, an' the throops are wantin' their dinner." He put his arm round av me an I came into the sun, the hills an' the rocks skippin' big giddy-go-rounds. "Seventeen years have I been in the army," sez the sargint, "an' the days av mericles are not done. They'll be givin' us more pay next. Begad," he sez, "the brute knows you!"

Ould Obstructionist was screamin' like all possist whin I came up, an' I heard forty million men up the Tangi shoutin', "He knows him!" Thin the big thrunk came round me an' I was nigh faintin' wid weakness. "Are you well, Malachi?" I sez, givin' him the name he answered to in the lines. "Malachi, my son, are you well?" sez I, "for I am not." At that he thrumpeted again till the Pass rang to ut, an' the other elephints tuk it up. Thin I got a little strength back. "Down, Malachi," I sez, "an' put me up, but touch me tendher for I am not good." He was on his knees in a minut' an' he slung me up as gentle as a girl. "Go on now, my son," I sez. "You're blockin' the road." He fetched wan more joyous toot, an' swung grand out av the head av the Tangi, his gun-gear clankin' on his back; an' at the back av him there wint the most amazin' shout I iver heard. An' thin I felt my head shpin, an' a mighty sweat bruk out on me, an' Malachi was growin' taller an' taller to me settin' on his back, an' I sez, foolish like an' weak, smilin' all round an' about, "Take me down," I sez, "or I'll fall."

'The next I remimber was lyin' in my cot again, limp as a chewed rag, but cured av the fever, an' the Tangi as empty as the back av my hand. They'd all gone up to the front, an' ten days later I wint up too, havin' blocked an' unblocked an entire Army Corps. What do you think av ut, sorr?'

'I'll wait till I see Learoyd,' I repeated.

'Ah'm here,' said a shadow from among the shadows. 'Ah've heeard t' tale too.'

'Is it true, Jock?'

'Ay; true as t'owd bitch has getten t'mange. Orth'ris, yo' maun't let t'dawgs hev owt to do wi' her.'

I KEEP SIX HONEST SERVING-MEN

I keep six honest serving-men
(They taught me all I knew);
Their names are What and Why and When
And How and Where and Who.
I send them over land and sea,
I send them east and west;
But after they have worked for me,
I give them all a rest.

I let them rest from nine till five,
For I am busy then,
As well as breakfast, lunch, and tea,
For they are hungry men:
But different folk have different views;
I know a person small –
She keeps ten million serving-men,
Who get no rest at all!
She sends 'em abroad on her own affairs,
From the second she opens her eyes –
One million Hows, two million Wheres,
And seven million Whys!

RIKKI-TIKKI-TAVI

At the hole where he went in
Red-Eye called to Wrinkle-Skin.
Hear what little Red-Eye saith:
'Nag, come up and dance with death!
Eye to eye and head to head,
  (*Keep the measure, Nag.*)
This shall end when one is dead;
  (*At thy pleasure, Nag.*)
Turn for turn and twist for twist –
  (*Run and hide thee, Nag.*)
Hah! The hooded Death has missed!
  (*Woe betide thee, Nag!*)

This is the story of the great war that Rikki-tikki-tavi fought single-handed, through the bath-rooms of the big bungalow in Segowlee cantonment. Darzee, the tailor-bird, helped him, and Chuchundra, the musk-rat, who never comes out into the middle of the floor, but always creeps round by the wall, gave him advice; but Rikki-tikki did the real fighting.

He was a mongoose, rather like a little cat in his fur and his tail, but quite like a weasel in his head and his habits. His eyes and the end of his restless nose were pink; he could scratch himself anywhere he pleased, with any leg, front or back, that he chose to use; he could fluff up his tail till it looked like a bottle-brush, and his war-cry, as he scuttled through the long grass, was: '*Rikk-tikk-tikki-tikki-tchk!*'

One day, a high summer flood washed him out of the burrow where he lived with his father and mother, and carried him, kicking and clucking, down a roadside ditch. He found a little wisp of grass floating there, and clung to it till he lost his senses. When he revived, he was lying in the hot sun on the middle of a garden path, very draggled indeed, and a small boy was saying: 'Here's a dead mongoose. Let's have a funeral.'

'No,' said his mother; 'let's take him in and dry him. Perhaps he isn't really dead.'

They took him into the house, and a big man picked him up between his finger and thumb, and said he was not dead but half choked; so they wrapped him in cotton-wool, and warmed him, and he opened his eyes and sneezed.

'Now,' said the big man (he was an Englishman who had just moved into the bungalow), 'don't frighten him, and we'll see what he'll do.'

It is the hardest thing in the world to frighten a mongoose, because he is eaten up from nose to tail with curiosity. The motto of all the mongoose family is 'Run and find out'; and Rikki-tikki was a true mongoose. He looked at the cotton-wool, decided that it was not good to eat, ran all round the table, sat up and put his fur in order, scratched himself, and jumped on the small boy's shoulder.

'Don't be frightened, Teddy,' said his father. 'That's his way of making friends.'

'Ouch! He's tickling under my chin,' said Teddy.

Rikki-tikki looked down between the boy's collar and neck, snuffed at his ear, and climbed down to the floor, where he sat rubbing his nose.

'Good gracious,' said Teddy's mother, 'and that's a wild creature! I suppose he's so tame because we've been kind to him.'

'All mongooses are like that,' said her husband. 'If Teddy doesn't pick him up by the tail, or try to put him in a cage, he'll run in and out of the house all day long. Let's give him something to eat.'

They gave him a little piece of raw meat. Rikki-tikki liked it immensely, and when it was finished he went out into the veranda and sat in the sunshine and fluffed up his fur to make it dry to the roots. Then he felt better.

'There are more things to find out about in this house,' he said to himself, 'than all my family could find out in all their lives. I shall certainly stay and find out.'

He spent all that day roaming over the house. He nearly drowned himself in the bath-tubs, put his nose into the ink on a writing-table, and burnt it on the end of the big man's cigar, for he climbed up in the big man's lap to see how writing was done. At nightfall he ran into Teddy's nursery to watch how kerosene lamps were lighted, and when Teddy went to bed Rikki-tikki climbed up too; but he was a restless companion, because he had to get up and attend to every noise all through the night, and find out what made it. Teddy's mother and father came in, the last thing, to look at their boy, and Rikki-tikki was awake on the pillow 'I don't like that,' said Teddy's mother; 'he may bite the child.' 'He'll do no such thing,' said the father. 'Teddy's safer with that little beast than if he had a bloodhound to watch him. If a snake came into the nursery now–'

But Teddy's mother wouldn't think of anything so awful.

Early in the morning Rikki-tikki came to early breakfast in the veranda riding on Teddy's shoulder, and they gave him banana and some boiled egg; and he sat on all their laps one after the other, because every well-brought-up mongoose always hopes to be a house-mongoose some day and have rooms to run about in, and Rikki-tikki's mother (she used to live in the General's house at

Segowlee) had carefully told Rikki what to do if ever he came across white men.

Then Rikki-tikki went out into the garden to see what was to be seen. It was a large garden, only half cultivated, with bushes as big as summer-houses of Marshal Niel roses, lime and orange trees, clumps of bamboos, and thickets of high grass. Rikki-tikki licked his lips. 'This is a splendid hunting-ground,' he said, and his tail grew bottle-brushy at the thought of it, and he scuttled up and down the garden, snuffing here and there till he heard very sorrowful voices in a thorn-bush.

It was Darzee, the tailor-bird, and his wife. They had made a beautiful nest by pulling two big leaves together and stitching them up the edges with fibres, and had filled the hollow with cotton and downy fluff. The nest swayed to and fro, as they sat on the rim and cried.

'What is the matter?' asked Rikki-tikki.

'We are very miserable,' said Darzee. 'One of our babies fell out of the nest yesterday, and Nag ate him.'

'H'm!' said Rikki-tikki, 'that is very sad – but I am a stranger here. Who is Nag?'

Darzee and his wife only cowered down in the nest without answering, for from the thick grass at the foot of the bush there came a low hiss – a horrid cold sound that made Rikki-tikki jump back two clear feet.

Then inch by inch out of the grass rose up the head and spread hood of Nag, the big black cobra, and he was five feet long from tongue to tail. When he had lifted one-third of himself clear of the ground, he stayed balancing to and fro exactly as a dandelion-tuft balances in the wind, and he looked at Rikki-tikki with the wicked snake's eyes that never change their expression, whatever the snake may be thinking of.

'Who is Nag?' said he. 'I am Nag. The great god Brahm put his mark upon all our people when the first cobra spread his hood to keep the sun off Brahm as he slept. Look, and be afraid!'

He spread out his hood more than ever, and Rikki-tikki saw the spectacle-mark on the back of it that looks exactly like the eye part of a hook-and-eye fastening. He was afraid for the minute; but it is impossible for a mongoose to stay frightened for any length of time, and though Rikki-tikki had never met a live cobra before, his mother had fed him on dead ones, and he knew that all a grown mongoose's business in life was to fight and eat snakes. Nag knew that too, and at the bottom of his cold heart he was afraid.

'Well,' said Rikki-tikki, and his tail began to fluff up again, 'marks or no marks, do you think it is right for you to eat fledglings out of a nest?'

Nag was thinking to himself, and watching the least little movement in the grass behind Rikki-tikki. He knew that mongooses in the garden meant death sooner or later for him and his family, but he wanted to get Rikki-tikki off his guard. So he dropped his head a little, and put it on one side.

'Let us talk,' he said. 'You eat eggs. Why should not I eat birds?'

'Behind you! Look behind you!' sang Darzee.

Rikki-tikki knew better than to waste time in staring. He jumped up in the air as high as he could go, and just under him whizzed by the head of Nagaina, Nag's wicked wife. She had crept up behind him as he was talking, to make an end of him; and he heard her savage hiss as the stroke missed. He came down almost across her back, and if he had been an old mongoose he would have known that then was the time to break her back with one bite but he was afraid of the terrible lashing return-stroke of the cobra. He bit, indeed, but did not bite long enough, and he jumped clear of the whisking tail, leaving Nagaina torn and angry.

'Wicked, wicked Darzee!' said Nag, lashing up as high as he could reach toward the nest in the thorn-bush; but Darzee had built it out of reach of snakes, and it only swayed to and fro.

Rikki-tikki felt his eyes growing red and

hot (when a mongoose s eyes grow red, he is angry), and he sat back on his tail and hind legs like a little kangaroo, and looked all round him, and chattered with rage. But Nag and Nagaina had disappeared into the grass. When a snake misses its stroke, it never says anything or gives any sign of what it means to do next. Rikki-tikki did not care to follow them, for he did not feel sure that he could manage two snakes at once. So he trotted off to the gravel path near the house, and sat down to think. It was a serious matter for him.

If you read the old books of natural history, you will find they say that when the mongoose fights the snake and happens to get bitten, he runs off and eats some herb that cures him. That is not true. The victory is only a matter of quickness of eye and quickness of foot, – snake's blow against mongoose's jump, – and as no eye can follow the motion of a snake's head when it strikes, that makes things much more wonderful than any magic herb. Rikki-tikki knew he was a young mongoose, and it made him all the more pleased to think that he had managed to escape a blow from behind. It gave him confidence in himself, and when Teddy came running down the path, Rikki-tikki was ready to be petted.

But just as Teddy was stooping, something flinched a little in the dust, and a tiny voice said: 'Be careful. I am death!' It was Karait, the dusty brown snakeling that lies for choice on the dusty earth; and his bite is as dangerous as the cobra's. But he is so small that nobody thinks of him, and so he does the more harm to people.

Rikki-tikki's eyes grew red again, and he danced up to Karait with the peculiar rocking, swaying motion that he had inherited from his family. It looks very funny, but it is so perfectly balanced a gait that you can fly off from it at any angle you please; and in dealing with snakes this is an advantage. If Rikki-tikki had only known, he was doing a much more dangerous thing than fighting Nag, for Karait is so small, and can turn so quickly, that unless Rikki bit him close to the back of the head, he would get the return-stroke in his eye or lip. But Rikki did not know: his eyes were all red, and he rocked back and forth, looking for a good place to hold. Karait struck out. Rikki jumped sideways and tried to run in, but the wicked little dusty grey head lashed within a fraction of his shoulder, and he had to jump over the body, and the head followed his heels close.

Teddy shouted to the house: 'Oh, look here! Our mongoose is killing a snake'; and Rikki-tikki heard a scream from Teddy's mother. His father ran out with a stick, but by the time he came up, Karait had lunged out once too far, and Rikki-tikki had sprung, jumped on the snake's back, dropped his head far between his forelegs, bitten as high up the back as he could get hold, and rolled away. That bite paralysed Karait, and Rikki-tikki was just going to eat him up from the tail, after the custom of his family at dinner, when he remembered that a full meal makes a slow mongoose, and if he wanted all his strength and quickness ready, he must keep himself thin.

He went away for a dust-bath under the castor-oil bushes, while Teddy's father beat the dead Karait. 'What is the use of that?' thought Rikki-tikki. 'I have settled it all'; and then Teddy's mother picked him up from the dust and hugged him, crying that he had saved Teddy from death, and Teddy's father said that he was a providence, and Teddy looked on with big scared eyes. Rikki-tikki was rather amused at all the fuss, which, of course, he did not understand. Teddy's mother might just as well have petted Teddy for playing in the dust. Rikki was thoroughly enjoying himself.

That night, at dinner, walking to and fro among the wineglasses on the table, he could have stuffed himself three times over with nice things; but he remembered Nag and Nagaina, and though it was very pleasant to be patted and petted by Teddy's mother, and to sit on Teddy's shoulder, his eyes would get red from time to time, and he would go off into his long war-cry of *'Rikk-tikki-tikki-tikki-tchk!'*

Teddy carried him off to bed, and insisted on Rikki-tikki sleeping under his chin. Rikki-tikki was too well bred to bite or scratch, but as soon as Teddy was asleep he went off for his nightly walk round the house, and in the dark he ran up against Chuchundra, the musk-rat, creeping round by the wall. Chuchundra is a broken-hearted little beast. He whimpers and cheeps all the night, trying to make up his mind to run into the middle of the room, but he never gets there.

'Don't kill me,' said Chuchundra, almost weeping. 'Rikki-tikki, don't kill me.'

'Do you think a snake-killer kills musk-rats?' said Rikki-tikki scornfully.

'Those who kill snakes get killed by snakes,' said Chuchundra, more sorrowfully than ever. 'And how am I to be sure that Nag won't mistake me for you some dark night?'

'There's not the least danger,' said Rikki-tikki; 'but Nag is in the garden, and I know you don't go there.'

'My cousin Chua, the rat, told me—' said Chuchundra, and then he stopped.

'Told you what?'

'H'sh! Nag is everywhere, Rikki-tikki. You should have talked to Chua in the garden.'

'I didn't – so you must tell me. Quick, Chuchundra, or I'll bite you!'

Chuchundra sat down and cried till the tears rolled off his whiskers. 'I am a very poor man,' he sobbed. 'I never had spirit enough to run out into the middle of the room. H'sh! I mustn't tell you anything. Can't you *hear*, Rikki-tikki?'

Rikki-tikki listened. The house was as still as still, but he thought he could just catch the faintest *scratch-scratch* in the world – a noise as faint as that of a wasp walking on a windowpane, – the dry scratch of a snake's scales on brickwork.

'That's Nag or Nagaina,' he said to himself; 'and he is crawling into the bath-room sluice. You're right, Chuchundra; I should have talked to Chua.'

He stole off to Teddy's bath-room, but there was nothing there, and then to Teddy's mother's bath-room. At the bottom of the smooth plaster wall there was a brick pulled out to make a sluice for the bath-water, and as Rikki-tikki stole in by the masonry curb where the bath is put, he heard Nag and Nagaina whispering together outside in the moonlight.

'When the house is emptied of people,' said Nagaina to her husband, '*he* will have to go away, and then the garden will be our own again. Go in quietly, and remember that the big man who killed Karait is the first one to bite. Then come out and tell me, and we will hunt for Rikki-tikki together.'

'But are you sure that there is anything to be gained by killing the people?' said Nag.

'Everything. When there were no people in the bungalow, did we have any mongoose in the garden? So long as the bungalow is empty, we are king and queen of the garden; and remember that as soon as our eggs in the melon-bed hatch (as they may to-morrow), our children will need room and quiet.'

'I had not thought of that,' said Nag. 'I will go, but there is no need that we should hunt for Rikki-tikki afterward. I will kill the big man and his wife, and the child if I can, and come away quietly. Then the bungalow will be empty, and Rikki-tikki will go.'

Rikki-tikki tingled all over with rage and hatred at this, and then Nag's head came through the sluice, and his five feet of cold body followed it. Angry as he was, Rikki-tikki was very frightened as he saw the size of the big cobra. Nag coiled himself up, raised his head, and looked into the bath-room in the dark, and Rikki could see his eyes glitter.

'Now, if I kill him here, Nagaina will know; and if I fight him on the open floor, the odds are in his favour. What am I to do?' said Rikki-tikki-tavi.

Nag waved to and fro, and then Rikki-tikki

heard him drinking from the biggest water-jar that was used to fill the bath. 'That is good,' said the snake. 'Now, when Karait was killed, the big man had a stick. He may have that stick still, but when he comes in to bathe in the morning he will not have a stick. I shall wait here till he comes. Nagaina – do you hear me? – I shall wait here in the cool till daytime.'

There was no answer from outside, so Rikki-tikki knew Nagaina had gone away. Nag coiled himself down, coil by coil, round the bulge at the bottom of the water-jar, and Rikki-tikki stayed still as death. After an hour he began to move, muscle by muscle, toward the jar. Nag was asleep, and Rikki-tikki looked at his big back, wondering which would be the best place for a good hold. 'If I don't break his back at the first jump,' said Rikki, 'he can still fight; and if he fights – O Rikki!' He looked at the thickness of the neck below the hood, but that was too much for him; and a bite near the tail would only make Nag savage.

'It must be the head,' he said at last; 'the head above the hood; and when I am once there, I must not let go.'

Then he jumped. The head was lying a little clear of the waterjar, under the curve of it; and, as his teeth met, Rikki braced his back against the bulge of the red earthenware to hold down the head. This gave him just one second's purchase, and he made the most of it. Then he was battered to and fro as a rat is shaken by a dog to and fro on the floor, up and down, and round in great circles; but his eyes were red, and he held on as the body cart-whipped over the floor, upsetting the tin dipper and the soap-dish and the flesh-brush, and banged against the tin side of the bath. As he held he closed his jaws tighter and tighter, for he made sure he would be banged to death, and, for the honour of his family, he preferred to be found with his teeth locked. He was dizzy, aching, and felt shaken to pieces when something went off like a thunderclap just behind him; a hot wind knocked him senseless, and red fire singed his fur. The big man had been wakened by the noise, and had fired both barrels of a shot-gun into Nag just behind the hood.

Rikki-tikki held on with his eyes shut, for now he was quite sure he was dead; but the head did not move, and the big man picked him up and said: 'It's the mongoose again, Alice; the little chap has saved *our* lives now.' Then Teddy's mother came in with a very white face, and saw what was left of Nag, and Rikki-tikki dragged himself to Teddy's bedroom and spent half the rest of the night shaking himself tenderly to find out whether he really was broken into forty pieces, as he fancied.

When morning came he was very stiff, but well pleased with his doings. 'Now I have Nagaina to settle with, and she will be worse than five Nags, and there's no knowing when the eggs she spoke of will hatch. Goodness! I must go and see Darzee,' he said.

Without waiting for breakfast, Rikki-tikki ran to the thornbush where Darzee was singing a song of triumph at the top of his voice. The news of Nag's death was all over the garden, for the sweeper had thrown the body on the rubbish-heap.

'Oh, you stupid tuft of feathers!' said Rikki-tikki angrily. 'Is this the time to sing?'

'Nag is dead – is dead – is dead!' sang Darzee. 'The valiant Rikki-tikki caught him by the head and held fast. The big man brought the bang-stick, and Nag fell in two pieces! He will never eat my babies again.'

'All that's true enough; but where's Nagaina?' said Rikki-tikki, looking carefully round him.

'Nagaina came to the bathroom sluice and called for Nag,' Darzee went on; 'and Nag came out on the end of a stick – the sweeper picked him up on the end of a stick and threw him upon the rubbish-heap. Let us sing about the great, the red-eyed Rikki-tikki!' and Darzee filled his throat and sang.

'If I could get up to your nest, I'd roll all your babies out!' said Rikki-tikki. 'You don't know when to do the right thing at the right time. You're safe enough in your nest there, but it's war for me down here. Stop singing a minute, Darzee.'

'For the great, the beautiful Rikki-tikki's sake I will stop,' said Darzee. 'What is it, O Killer of the terrible Nag?'

'Where is Nagaina, for the third time?'

'On the rubbish-heap by the stables, mourning for Nag. Great is Rikki-tikki with the white teeth.'

'Bother my white teeth! Have you ever heard where she keeps her eggs?'

'In the melon-bed, on the end nearest the wall, where the sun strikes nearly all day. She hid them there weeks ago.'

'And you never thought it worth while to tell me? The end nearest the wall, you said?'

'Rikki-tikki, you are not going to eat her eggs?'

'Not eat exactly; no. Darzee, if you have a grain of sense you will fly off to the stables and pretend that your wing is broken, and let Nagaina chase you away to this bush. I must get to the melon-bed, and if I went there now she'd see me.'

Darzee was a feather-brained little fellow who could never hold more than one idea at a time in his head; and just because he knew that Nagaina's children were born in eggs like his own, he didn't think at first that it was fair to kill them. But his wife was a sensible bird, and she knew that cobra's eggs meant young cobras later on so she flew off from the nest, and left Darzee to keep the babies warm, and continue his song about the death of Nag. Darzee was very like a man in some ways.

She fluttered in front of Nagaina by the rubbish-heap, and cried out, 'Oh, my wing is broken! The boy in the house threw a stone at me and broke it.' Then she fluttered more desperately than ever.

Nagaina lifted up her head and hissed. 'You warned Rikki-tikki when I would have killed him. Indeed and truly, you've chosen a bad place to be lame in.' And she moved toward Darzee's wife, slipping along over the dust.

'The boy broke it with a stone!' shrieked Darzee's wife.

'Well! It may be some consolation to you when you're dead to know that I shall settle accounts with the boy. My husband lies on the rubbish-heap this morning, but before night the boy in the house will lie very still. What is the use of running away? I am sure to catch you. Little fool, look at me!'

Darzee's wife knew better than to do *that*, for a bird who looks at a snake's eyes gets so frightened that she cannot move. Darzee's wife fluttered on, piping sorrowfully, and never leaving the ground, and Nagaina quickened her pace.

Rikki-tikki heard them going up the path from the stables:, and he raced for the end of the melon-patch near the wall. There, in the warm litter about the melons, very cunningly hidden, he found twenty-five eggs, about the size of a bantam's eggs, but with whitish skin instead of shell.

'I was not a day too soon,' he said; for he could see the baby cobras curled up inside the skin, and he knew that the minute they were hatched they could each kill a man or a mongoose. He bit off the tops of the eggs as fast as he could, taking care to crush the young cobras, and turned over the litter from time to time to see whether he had missed any. At last there were only three eggs left, and Rikki-tikki began to chuckle to himself, when he heard Darzee's wife screaming:

'Rikki-tikki, I led Nagaina toward the house, and she has gone into the veranda, and – oh, come quickly – she means killing!'

Rikki-tikki smashed two eggs, and tumbled backward down the melon-bed with the third egg in his mouth, and scuttled to the veranda as hard as he could put foot to the ground. Teddy and his mother and father were there at early breakfast; but Rikki-tikki saw that they were not eating anything. They sat stone-still, and their faces were white. Nagaina was coiled up on the matting by Teddy's chair, within easy striking-distance of Teddy's bare leg, and she was swaying to and fro singing a song of triumph.

'Son of the big man that killed Nag,' she hissed, 'stay still. I am not ready yet. Wait a little. Keep very still, all you three. If you move I strike, and if you do not move I strike. Oh, foolish people, who killed my Nag!'

Teddy's eyes were fixed on his father, and all his father could do was to whisper, 'Sit still, Teddy. You mustn't move. Teddy, keep still.'

Then Rikki-tikki came up and cried: 'Turn round, Nagaina; turn and fight!'

'All in good time,' said she, without moving her eyes. 'I will settle my account with you presently. Look at your friends, Rikki-tikki. They are still and white; they are afraid. They dare not move, and if you come a step nearer I strike.'

'Look at your eggs,' said Rikki-tikki, 'in the melon-bed near the wall. Go and look, Nagaina.'

The big snake turned half round, and saw the egg on the veranda.

'Ah-h! Give it to me,' she said.

Rikki-tikki put his paws one on each side of the egg, and his eyes were blood-red. 'What price for a snake's egg? For a young cobra? For a young king-cobra? For the last – the very last of the brood? The ants are eating all the others down by the melon-bed.'

Nagaina spun clear round, forgetting

everything for the sake of the one egg; and Rikki-tikki saw Teddy's father shoot out a big hand, catch Teddy by the shoulder, and drag him across the little table with the tea-cups, safe and out of reach of Nagaina.

'Tricked! Tricked! Tricked! *Rikk-tck-tck!*' chuckled Rikki-tikki. 'The boy is safe, and it was I – I – I that caught Nag by the hood last night in the bath-room.' Then he began to jump up and down, all four feet together, his head close to the floor. 'He threw me to and fro, but he could not shake me off. He was dead before the big man blew him in two. I did it. *Rikki-tikki-tck-tck!* Come then, Nagaina. Come and fight with me. You shall not be a widow long.'

Nagaina saw that she had lost her chance of killing Teddy, and the egg lay between Rikki-tikki's paws. 'Give me the egg, Rikki-tikki. Give me the last of my eggs, and I will go away and never come back,' she said, lowering her hood.

'Yes, you will go away, and you will never come back; for you will go to the rubbish-heap with Nag. Fight, widow! The big man has gone for his gun! Fight!'

Rikki-tikki was bounding all round Nagaina, keeping just out of reach of her stroke, his little eyes like hot coals. Nagaina gathered herself together, and flung out at him. Rikki-tikki jumped up and backward. Again and again and again she struck, and each time her head came with a whack on the matting of the veranda, and she gathered herself together like a watch-spring. Then Rikki-tikki danced in a circle to get behind her, and Nagaina spun round to keep her head to his head, so that the rustle of her tail on the matting sounded like dry leaves blown along by the wind.

He had forgotten the egg. It still lay on the veranda, and Nagaina came nearer and nearer to it, till at last, while Rikki-tikki was drawing breath, she caught it in her mouth, turned to the veranda steps, and flew like an arrow down the path, with Rikki-tikki behind her. When the cobra runs for her life, she goes like a whiplash flicked across a horse's neck.

Rikki-tikki knew that he must catch her, or all the trouble would begin again. She headed straight for the long grass by the thorn-bush, and as he was running Rikki-tikki heard Darzee still singing his foolish little song of triumph. But Darzee's wife was wiser. She flew off her nest as Nagaina came along, and flapped her wings about Nagaina's head. If Darzee had helped they might have turned her; but Nagaina only lowered her hood and went on. Still, the instant's delay brought Rikki-tikki up to her, and as she plunged into the rat-hole where she and Nag used to live, his little white teeth were clenched on her tail, and he went down with her – and very few mongooses, however wise and old they may be, care to follow a cobra into its hole. It was dark in the hole; and Rikki-tikki never knew when it might open out and give Nagaina room to turn and strike at him. He held on savagely, and stuck out his feet to act as brakes on the dark slope of the hot, moist earth.

Then the grass by the mouth of the hole stopped waving, and Darzee said: 'It is all over with Rikki-tikki! We must sing his death-song. Valiant Rikki-tikki is dead! For Nagaina will surely kill him underground.'

So he sang a very mournful song that he made up on the spur of the minute, and just as he got to the most touching part the grass quivered again, and Rikki-tikki, covered with dirt, dragged himself out of the hole leg by leg, licking his whiskers. Darzee stopped with a little shout. Rikki-tikki shook some of the dust out of his fur and sneezed. 'It is all over,' he said. 'The widow will never come out again.' And the red ants that live between the grass stems heard him, and began to troop down one after another to see if he had spoken the truth.

Rikki-tikki curled himself up in the grass and slept where he was – slept and slept till it was late in the afternoon, for he had done a hard day's work.

'Now,' he said, when he awoke, 'I will go back to the house. Tell the Coppersmith,

Darzee, and he will tell the garden that Nagaina is dead.'

The Coppersmith is a bird who makes a noise exactly like the beating of a little hammer on a copper pot; and the reason he is always making it is because he is the town-crier to every Indian garden, and tells all the news to everybody who cares to listen. As Rikki-tikki went up the path, he heard his 'attention' notes like a tiny dinner-gong; and then the steady *'Ding-dong-tock! Nag is dead – dong! Nagaina is dead! Ding-dong-tock!'* That set all the birds in the garden singing, and the frogs croaking; for Nag and Nagaina used to eat frogs as well as little birds.

When Rikki got to the house, Teddy and Teddy's mother (she still looked very white, for she had been fainting) and Teddy's father came out and almost cried over him; and that night he ate all that was given him till he could eat no more, and went to bed on Teddy's shoulder, where Teddy's mother saw him when she came to look late at night.

'He saved our lives and Teddy's life,' she said to her husband. 'Just think, he saved all our lives!'

Rikki-tikki woke up with a jump, for all the mongooses are light sleepers.

'Oh, it's you,' said he. 'What are you bothering for? All the cobras are dead; and if they weren't, I'm here.'

Rikki-tikki had a right to be proud of himself; but he did not grow too proud, and he kept that garden as a mongoose should keep it, with tooth and jump and spring and bite, till never a cobra dared show its head inside the walls.

DARZEE'S CHAUNT
(SUNG IN HONOUR OF
RIKKI-TIKKI–TAVI)

Singer and tailor am I –
  Doubled the joys that I know –
Proud of my lilt through the sky,
  Proud of the house that I sew –
Over and under, so weave I my music – so
  weave I the house that I sew.
Sing to your fledglings again,
  Mother, oh, lift up your head!
Evil that plagued us is slain,
  Death in the garden lies dead.
Terror that hid in the roses is impotent –
  flung on the dung-hill and dead!
Who hath delivered us, who?
  Tell me his nest and his name.
Rikki, the valiant, the true,
  Tikki, with eyeballs of flame,
Rik-tikki-tikki, the ivory-fangéd, the
  hunter with eyeballs of flame.

Give him the Thanks of the Birds,
  Bowing with tail-feathers spread!
Praise him with nightingale-words –
  Nay, I will praise him instead.
Hear! I will sing you the praise of the

bottle-tailed Rikki, with eyeballs of red!

*(Here Rikki-tikki interrupted, and the rest of
the song is lost.)*

MOTI GUJ – MUTINEER

Once upon a time there was a coffee-planter in India who wished to clear some forest land for coffee-planting. When he had cut down all the trees and burned the under-wood the stumps still remained. Dynamite is expensive and slow-fire slow. The happy medium for stump-clearing is the lord of all beasts, who is the elephant. He will either push the stump out of the ground with his tusks, if he has any, or drag it out with ropes. The planter, therefore, hired elephants by ones and twos and threes, and fell to work. The very best of all the elephants belonged to the very worst of all the drivers or mahouts; and the superior beast's name was Moti Guj. He was the absolute property of his mahout, which would never have been the case under native rule, for Moti Guj was a creature to be desired by kings; and his name, being translated, meant the Pearl Elephant. Because the British Government was in the land, Deesa, the mahout, enjoyed his property undisturbed. He was dissi-pated. When he had made much money through the strength of his elephant, he would get extremely drunk and give Moti

Guj a beating with a tent-peg over the tender nails of the forefeet. Moti Guj never trampled the life out of Deesa on these occasions, for he knew that after the beating was over Deesa would embrace his trunk, and weep and call him his love and his life and the liver of his soul, and give him some liquor. Moti Guj was very fond of liquor – arrack for choice, though he would drink palm-tree toddy if nothing better offered. Then Deesa would go to sleep between Moti Guj's forefeet, and as Deesa generally chose the middle of the public road, and as Moti Guj mounted guard over him and would not permit horse, foot, or cart to pass by, traffic was congested till Deesa saw fit to wake up.

There was no sleeping in the daytime on the planter's clearing: the wages were too high to risk. Deesa sat on Moti Guj's neck and gave him orders, while Moti Guj rooted up the stumps – for he owned a magnificent pair of tusks; or pulled at the end of a rope – for he had a magnificent pair of shoulders, while Deesa kicked him behind the ears and said he was the king of elephants. At evening time Moti Guj would wash down his three hundred pounds' weight of green food with a quart of arrack, and Deesa would take a share and sing songs between Moti Guj's legs till it was time to go to bed. Once a week Deesa led Moti Guj down to the river, and Moti Guj lay on his side luxuriously in the shallows, while Deesa went over him with a coir-swab and a brick. Moti Guj never mistook the pounding blow of the latter for the smack of the former that warned him to get up and turn over on the other side. Then Deesa would look at his feet, and examine his eyes, and turn up the fringes of his mighty ears in case of sores or budding ophthalmia. After inspection, the two would 'come up with a song from the sea,' Moti Guj all black and shining, waving a torn tree branch twelve feet long in his trunk, and Deesa knotting up his own long wet hair.

It was a peaceful, well-paid life till Deesa felt the return of the desire to drink deep. He wished for an orgy. The little draughts that led nowhere were taking the manhood out of him.

He went to the planter, and 'My mother's dead,' said he, weeping.

'She died on the last plantation two months ago; and she died once before that when you were working for me last year,' said the planter, who knew something of the ways of nativedom.

'Then it's my aunt, and she was just the same as a mother to me,' said Deesa, weeping more than ever. 'She has left eighteen small children entirely without bread, and it is I who must fill their little stomachs,' said

Deesa, beating his head on the floor.

'Who brought you the news?' said the planter.

'The post,' said Deesa.

'There hasn't been a post here for the past week. Get back to your lines!'

'A devastating sickness has fallen on my village, and all my wives are dying,' yelled Deesa, really in tears this time.

'Call Chihun, who comes from Deesa's village,' said the planter. 'Chihun, has this man a wife?'

'He!' said Chihun. 'No. Not a woman of our village would look at him. They'd sooner marry the elephant.' Chihun snorted. Deesa wept and bellowed.

'You will get into a difficulty in a minute,' said the planter. 'Go back to your work!'

'Now I will speak Heaven's truth,' gulped Deesa, with an inspiration. 'I haven't been drunk for two months. I desire to depart in order to get properly drunk afar off and distant from this heavenly plantation. Thus I shall cause no trouble.'

A flickering smile crossed the planter's face. 'Deesa,' said he, 'you've spoken the truth, and I'd give you leave on the spot if anything could be done with Moti Guj while you're away. You know that he will only obey your orders.'

'May the Light of the Heavens live forty thousand years. I shall be absent but ten little days. After that, upon my faith and honour and soul, I return. As to the inconsiderable interval, have I the gracious permission of the Heaven-born to call up Moti Guj?'

Permission was granted, and, in answer to Deesa's shrill yell, the lordly tusker swung out of the shade of a clump of trees where he had been squirting dust over himself till his master should return.

'Light of my heart, Protector of the Drunken, Mountain of Might, give ear,' said Deesa, standing in front of him.

Moti Guj gave ear, and saluted with his trunk. 'I am going away,' said Deesa.

Moti Guj's eyes twinkled. He liked jaunts as well as his master. One could snatch all manner of nice things from the roadside then.

'But you, you fubsy old pig, must stay behind and work.'

The twinkle died out as Moti Guj tried to look delighted. He hated stump-hauling on the plantation. It hurt his teeth.

'I shall be gone for ten days, O Delectable One. Hold up your near forefoot and I'll impress the fact upon it, warty toad of a dried mud-puddle.' Deesa took a tent-peg and banged Moti Guj ten times on the nails. Moti Guj grunted and shuffled from foot to foot.

'Ten days,' said Deesa, 'you must work

243

and haul and root trees as Chihun here shall order you. Take up Chihun and set him on your neck!' Moti Guj curled the tip of his trunk, Chihun put his foot there and was swung on to the neck. Deesa handed Chihun the heavy *ankus*, the iron elephant-goad.

Chihun thumped Moti Guj's bald head as a paviour thumps a kerbstone.

Moti Guj trumpeted.

'Be still, hog of the backwoods! Chihun's your mahout for ten days. And now bid me goodbye, beast after mine own heart. Oh, my lord, my king! Jewel of all created elephants, lily of the herd, preserve your honoured health; be virtuous. Adieu!'

Moti Guj lapped his trunk round Deesa and swung him into the air twice. That was his way of bidding the man goodbye.

'He'll work now,' said Deesa to the planter. 'Have I leave to go?'

The planter nodded, and Deesa dived into the woods. Moti Guj went back to haul stumps.

Chihun was very kind to him, but he felt unhappy and forlorn notwithstanding. Chihun gave him balls of spices, and tickled him under the chin, and Chihun's little baby cooed to him after work was over, and Chihun's wife called him a darling; but Moti Guj was a bachelor by instinct, as Deesa was. He did not understand the domestic emotions. He wanted the light of his universe back again – the drink and the drunken slumber, the savage beatings and the savage caresses.

None the less he worked well, and the planter wondered. Deesa had vagabonded along the roads till he met a marriage procession of his own caste and, drinking, dancing, and tippling, had drifted past all knowledge of the lapse of time.

The morning of the eleventh day dawned, and there returned no Deesa. Moti Guj was loosed from his ropes for the daily stint. He swung clear, looked round, shrugged his shoulders, and began to walk away, as one having business elsewhere.

'Hi! ho! Come back, you,' shouted Chihun. 'Come back, and put me on your neck, Misborn Mountain. Return, Splendour of the Hillsides. Adornment of all India, heave to, or I'll bang every toe off your fat forefoot!'

Moti Guj gurgled gently, but did not obey. Chihun ran after him with a rope and caught him up. Moti Guj put his ears forward, and Chihun knew what that meant, though he tried to carry it off with high words.

'None of your nonsense with me,' said he. 'To your pickets, Devil-son.'

'Hrrump!' said Moti Guj, and that was all – that and the forebent ears.

Moti Guj put his hands in his pockets,

chewed a branch for a toothpick, and strolled about the clearing, making jest of the other elephants, who had just set to work.

Chihun reported the state of affairs to the planter, who came out with a dog-whip and cracked it furiously. Moti Guj paid the white man the compliment of charging him nearly a quarter of a mile across the clearing and 'Hrrumphing' him into the veranda. Then he stood outside the house chuckling to himself, and shaking all over with the fun of it, as an elephant will.

'We'll thrash him,' said the planter. 'He shall have the finest thrashing that ever elephant received. Give Kala Nag and Nazim twelve foot of chain apiece, and tell them to lay on twenty blows.'

Kala Nag – which means Black Snake – and Nazim were two of the biggest elephants in the lines, and one of their duties was to administer the graver punishments, since no man can beat an elephant properly.

They took the whipping-chains and rattled them in their trunks as they sidled up to Moti Guj, meaning to hustle him between them. Moti Guj had never, in all his life of thirty-nine years, been whipped, and he did not intend to open new experiences. So he waited, weaving his head from right to left, and measuring the precise spot in Kala Nag's fat side where a blunt tusk would sink deepest. Kala Nag had no tusks; the chain was his badge of authority; but he judged it good to swing wide of Moti Guj at the last minute, and to appear as if he had brought out the chain for amusement. Nazim turned round and went home early. He did not feel fighting-fit that morning, and so Moti Guj was left standing alone with his ears cocked.

That decided the planter to argue no more, and Moti Guj rolled back to his inspection of the clearing. An elephant who will not work, and is not tied up, is not quite so manageable as an eighty-one ton gun loose in a heavy sea-way. He slapped old friends on the back and asked them if the stumps were coming away easily; he talked nonsense concerning labour and the inalienable rights of elephants to a long nooning; and, wandering to and fro, thoroughly demoralised the garden till sundown, when he returned to his pickets for food.

'If you won't work you shan't eat,' said Chihun angrily. 'You're a wild elephant, and no educated animal at all. Go back to your jungle.'

Chihun's little brown baby, rolling on the floor of the hut, stretched its fat arms to the huge shadow in the doorway. Moti Guj knew well that it was the dearest thing on earth to Chihun. He swung out his trunk with a fascinating crook at the end, and the brown baby threw itself shouting upon it. Moti Guj made fast and pulled up till the brown baby was crowing in the air twelve feet above his father's head.

'Great Chief!' said Chihun. 'Flour cakes of the best, twelve in number, two feet across, and soaked in rum shall be yours on the instant, and two hundred pounds' weight of fresh-cut young sugar cane therewith. Deign only to put down safely that insignificant brat who is my heart and my life to me.'

Moti Guj tucked the brown baby comfortably between his forefeet, that could have knocked into toothpicks all Chihun's hut, and waited for his food. He ate it, and the brown baby crawled away. Moti Guj dozed, and thought of Deesa. One of many mysteries connected with the elephant is that his huge body needs less sleep than anything else that lives. Four or five hours in the night suffice – two just before midnight, lying down on one side; two just after one o'clock, lying down on the other. The rest of the silent hours are filled with eating and fidgeting and long grumbling soliloquies.

At midnight, therefore, Moti Guj strode out of his pickets, for a thought had come to him that Deesa might be lying drunk somewhere in the dark forest with none to look after him. So all that night he chased through the undergrowth, blowing and trumpeting and shaking his ears. He went down to the river and blared across the shallows where Deesa used to wash him, but there was no answer. He could not find Deesa, but he disturbed all the elephants in the lines, and nearly frightened to death some gipsies in the woods.

At dawn Deesa returned to the plantation. He had been very drunk indeed, and he expected to fall into trouble for outstaying his leave. He drew a long breath when he saw that the bungalow and the plantation were still uninjured; for he knew something of Moti Guj's temper; and reported himself with many lies and salaams. Moti Guj had gone to his pickets for breakfast. His night exercise had made him hungry.

'Call up your beast,' said the planter, and Deesa shouted in the mysterious elephant-language, that some mahouts believe came from China at the birth of the world, when elephants and not men were masters. Moti Guj heard and came. Elephants do not gallop. They move from spots at varying rates of speed. If an elephant wished to catch an express train he could not gallop, but he could catch the train. Thus Moti Guj was at the planter's door almost before Chihun noticed that he had left his pickets. He fell into Deesa's arms trumpeting with joy, and the man and beast wept and slobbered over each other, and handled each other from head to heel to see that no harm had befallen.

'Now we will get to work,' said Deesa. 'Lift me up, my son and my joy.'

Moti Guj swung him up and the two went to the coffee-clearing to look for irksome stumps.

The planter was too astonished to be very angry.

I WILL REMEMBER WHAT I WAS

I will remember what I was. I am sick of
 rope and chain.
I will remember my old strength and all
 my forest affairs.
I will not sell my back to man for a bundle
 of sugar-cane,
I will go out to my own kind, and the
 woodfolk in their lairs.
I will go out until the day, until the
 morning break,
Out to the winds' untainted kiss, the
 waters' clean caress;
I will forget my ankle-ring and snap my
 picket-stake.
I will revisit my lost loves, and playmates
 masterless!

PRIVATE LEAROYD'S STORY
And he told a tale.

– Chronicles of Gautama Budha.

Far from the haunts of Company Officers who insist upon kit inspections, far from keen-nosed Sergeants who sniff the pipe stuffed into the bedding-roll, two miles from the tumult of the barracks, lies the Trap. It is an old dry well, shadowed by a twisted *pipal* tree and fenced with high grass. Here, in the years gone by, did Private Ortheris establish his depot and menagerie for such possessions, dead and living, as could not safely be introduced to the barrack-room. Here were gathered Houdin pullets, and fox-terriers of undoubted pedigree and more than doubtful ownership, for Ortheris was an inveterate poacher and pre-eminent among a regiment of neat-handed dog-stealers.

Never again will the long lazy evenings return wherein Ortheris, whistling softly, moved surgeon-wise among the captives of his craft at the bottom of the well; when Learoyd sat in the niche, giving sage counsel on the management of 'tykes,' and

Mulvaney, from the crook of the over-hanging *pipal* waved his enormous boots in benediction above our heads, delighting us with tales of Love and War, and strange experiences of cities and men.

Ortheris – landed at last in the 'little stuff' bird-shop for which your soul longed; Learoyd – back again in the smoky, stone-ribbed North, amid the clang of the Bradford looms; Mulvaney – grizzled, tender, and very wise Ulysses, sweltering on the earthwork of a Central India line – judge if I have forgotten old days in the Trap!...

Orth'ris, as allus thinks he knaws more than other foaks, said she wasn't a real laady, but nobbut a Hewrasian. I don't gainsay as her culler was a bit doosky like. But she *was* a laady. Why, she rode iv a carriage, an' good 'osses, too, an' her 'air was that oiled as you could see your faice in it, an' she wore di'mond rings an' a goold chain, an' silk an' satin dresses as mun a cost a deal, for it isn't a cheap shop as keeps enough o' one pattern to fit a figure like hers. Her name was Mrs DeSussa, an' t'waay I coom to be acquainted wi' her was along of our Colonel's Laady's dog Rip.

I've seen a vast o' dogs, but Rip was t'prettiest picter of a cliver fox-tarrier 'at iver I set eyes on. He could do owt you like but speeak, an' t' Colonel's Laady set more store by him than if he hed been a Christian. She hed bairns of her awn, but they was i' England, and Rip seemed to get all t'coodlin' an' pettin' as belonged to a bairn by good right.

But Rip were a bit on a rover, an' hed a habit o' breakin' out o' barricks like, and trottin' round t'plaice as if he were t' Cantonment Magistrate coom round inspectin'. The Colonel leathers him once or twice, but Rip didn't care an' kept on gooin' his rounds, wi' his taail a-waggin' as if he were flag-signallin' to t' world at large 'at he was 'gettin' on nicely, thank yo', and how's yo'sen?' An' then t' Colonel, as was noa sort of a hand wi' a dog, tees him oop. A real clipper of a dog, an' it's noa wonder yon laady, Mrs DeSussa, should tek a fancy tiv him. Theer's one o' t' Ten Commandments says yo' maun't cuvvet your neebor's ox nor his jackass, but it doesn't say nowt about his tarrier dogs, an' happen thot's t'reason why Mrs DeSussa cuvveted Rip, tho' she went to church reg'lar along wi' her husband, who was so mich darker 'at if he hedn't such a good coaat tiv his back yo' might ha' called him a black man and nut tell a lee nawther. They said he addled his brass i' jute, an' he'd a rare lot on it.

Well, yo' see, when they teed Rip oop, t' poor awd lad didn't enjoy very good 'ealth. So t' Colonel's Laady sends for me as 'ad a naame for bein' knowledgeable about a dog, an' axes what's ailin' wi' him.

'Why,' says I, 'he's getten t' mopes, an' what he wants is his libbaty an' coompany like t' rest on us; wal happen a rat or two 'ud liven him oop. It's low, mum,' says I, ''is rats, but it's t'nature of a dog; an' soa's cuttin' round an' meetin' another dog or two an' passin' t' time o' day, an' hevvin a bit of a turnup wi him like a Christian.'

So she says *her* dog maun't niver fight an' noa Christians iver fought.

'Then what's a soldier for?' says I; an' I explains to her t' contrairy qualities of a dog, 'at, when yo' coom to think on't, is one o' t' curusest things as is. For they larn to behave theirsens like gentlemen born, fit for t' fost o'coompany – they tell me Widdy herself is fond of a good dog and knaws one when she sees it as well as onny body: then on t'other hand a-tewin' round after cats an gettin' mixed oop i' all manners o blackguardly street-rows, an' killin' rats, an' fightin' like divils.

'T' Colonel's Laady says: – 'Well, Learoyd, I doan't agree wi' you, but you're right in a way o' speeakin', an' I should like yo' to tek Rip out a-walkin' wi' you sometimes; but yo' maun't let him fight, nor chase cats, nor do nowt 'orrid': an' them was her very wods.

Soa Rip an' me gooes out a-walkin' o' evenin's, he bein' a dog as did credit tiv a man, an' I catches a lot o' rats an' we hed a bit of a match on in an awd dry swimmin'-bath at back o' t' cantonments, an' it was none so long afore he was as bright as a button again. He hed a waay o' flyin' at them big yaller pariah dogs as if he was a harrow offan a bow, an' though his weight were nowt, he tuk 'em so suddint-like they rolled over like skittles in a halley, an' when they coot he stretched after 'em as if he were rabbit-runnin'. Saame wi cats when he cud get t' cat agaate o' runnin'.

One evenin', him an me was trespassin' ovver a compound wall after one of them mongooses 'at he'd started, an' we was busy grubbin' round a prickle-bush, an' when we looks oop there was Mrs DeSussa wi' a parasel ovver her shoulder, a-watchin' us. 'Oh my!' she sings out; 'there's that lovelee dog! Would he let me stroke him, Mister Soldier?'

'Ay, he would, mum,' says I, 'for he's fond o' laadies' coompany; Coom here, Rip, an' speeak to this kind laady.' An' Rip, seein' 'at t' mongoose hed getten clean awaay, cooms oop like t' gentleman he was, niver a hauporth shy nor okkord.

'Oh, you beautiful – you prettee dog!' she says, dippin' an' chantin' her speech in a waay them sooart has o' their awn; 'I would like a dog like you. You are so verree lovelee – so awfullee prettee,' an' all thot sort o' talk, 'at a dog o' sense mebbe thinks nowt on, tho' he bides it by reason o' his breedin'.

An' then I meks him joomp ovver my swagger-cane, an' shek hands, an' beg, an' lie dead, an' a lot o' them tricks as laadies teeaches dogs, though I doan't haud wi' it mysen; for it's makin' a fool o' a good dog to do such like.

An' at lung length it cooms out 'at she'd been thrawin' sheep's eyes, as t' sayin' is, at Rip for many a day. Yo' see, her childer was grown up, an' she'd nowt mich to do, an' were allus fond of a dog. Soa she axes me if I'd tek somethin' to dhrink. An' we goes into t' drawn-room wheer her 'usband was a-settin'. They meks a gurt fuss ovver t' dog an' I has a bottle o' aale an' he gave me a handful o' cigars.

Soa I coomed awaay, but t'awd lass sings out – 'Oh, Mister Soldier, please coom again and bring that prettee dog.'

I didn't let on to t' Colonel's Laady about Mrs DeSussa, an' Rip, he says nowt nawther; an' I gooes again, an' ivry time there was a good dhrink an' a handful o' good smooaks. An' I telled t' awd lass a heeap more about Rip than I'd iver heeard; how he tuk t'fost prize at Lunnon dog-show and cost thotty-three pounds fower shillin' from t'man as bred him; 'at his own brother was propputty o' t' Prince o' Wailes, an' 'at he had a pedigree as long as a Dook's. An' she lapped it all oop an' were niver tired o' admirin' him. But when t' awd lass took to givin' me money an' I seed 'at she were gettin' fair fond about t' dog, I began to suspicion summat. Onny body may give a soldier t' price of a pint in a friendly waay an' theer's no 'arm done, but when it cooms to five rupees slipt into your hand, sly like, why, it's what t' 'lectioneerin' fellows calls bribery an' corruption. Specially when Mrs DeSussa threwed hints how t'cold weather would soon be ovver, an' she was goin to Munsooree Pahar an' we was goin' to Rawalpindi, an' she would niver see Rip onny more onless somebody she knawed on would be kind tiv her.

Soa I tells Mulvaney an' Orth'ris all t' taale thro', beginnin' to end.

"Tis larceny that wicked ould laady manes,' says t' Irishman, "tis felony she is sejucin' ye into, my frind Learoyd, but I'll purtect your innocince. I'll save ye from the wicked wiles av that wealthy ould woman, an' I'll go wid ye this evenin and spake to her the wurrds av truth an' honesty. But, Jock,' says he, waggin' his heead, "twas not like ye to kape all that good dhrink an' thim fine cigars to yerself, while Orth'ris here an me have been prowlin' round wid throats as dry as lime-kims, and nothin' to smoke but Canteen plug. 'Twas a dhirty thrick to play on a comrade, for why should you, Learoyd,

258

be balancin' yerself on the butt av a satin chair, as if Terence Mulvaney was not the aquil av anybody who thrades in jute!'

'Let alone me,' sticks in Orth'ris, 'but that's like life. Them wot's really fitted to decorate society get no show, while a blunderin' Yorkshireman like you–'

'Nay,' says I, 'it's none o' t' blunderin' Yorkshireman she wants; it's Rip. He's t' gentleman this journey.'

Soa t' next day, Mulvaney an' Rip an' me goes to Mrs DeSussa's, an' t' Irishman bein' a strainger she wor a bit shy at fost. But yo've heeard Mulvaney talk, an' yo' may believe as he fairly bewitched t' awd lass wal she let out 'at she wanted to tek Rip awaay wi' her to Munsooree Pahar. Then Mulvaney changes his tune an' axes her solemn-like if she'd thought o' t' consequences o' gettin' two poor but honest soldiers sent t' Andamning Islands. Mrs DeSussa began to cry, so Mulvaney turns round oppen t'other tack and smooths her down, allowin' 'at Rip ud be a vast better off in t' Hills than down i' Bengal, and 'twas a pity he shouldn't go wheer he was so well beliked. And soa he went on, backin' an' fillin' an' workin' up t' awd lass wal she felt as if her life warn't worth nowt if she didn't hev t' dog.

Then all of a suddint he says: – 'But ye *shall* have him, marm, for I've a feelin' heart, not like this could-blooded Yorkshireman; but 'twill cost ye not a penny less than three hundher rupees.'

'Don't yo' believe him, mum,' says I; 't' Colonel's Laady wouldn't tek five hundred for him.'

'Who said she would?' says Mulvaney; 'it's not buyin' him I mane, but for the sake o' this kind, good laady, I'll do what I never dreamt to do in my life. I'll stale him!'

'Don't say steal,' says Mrs DeSussa; 'he shall have the happiest home. Dogs often get lost, you know, and then they stray, an' he likes me and I like him as I niver liked a dog yet, an' I *must* hev him. If I got him at t' last minute I could carry him off to Munsooree Pahar and nobody would niver knaw.'

Now an' again Mulvaney looked acrost at me, an' though I could mek nowt o' what he was after, I concluded to take his leead.

'Well, mum,' I says, 'I never thowt to coom down to dog-steealin', but if my comrade sees how it could be done to oblige a laady like yo'sen, I'm nut t' man to hod back, tho' it's a bad business I'm thinkin' an' three hundred rupees is a poor set-off again t'chance of them Damning Islands as Mulvaney talks on.'

'I'll mek it three-fifty,' says Mrs DeSussa; 'only let me hev t' dog!'

So we let her persuade us, an' she teks

Rip's measure theer an' then, an' sent to Hamilton's to order a silver collar again t' time when he was to be her awn, which was to be t' day she set off for Munsooree Pahar.

'Sitha, Mulvaney,' says I, when we was outside, 'you're niver goin' to let her hev Rip!'

'An' wud ye disappoint a poor old woman?' says he; 'she shall have a Rip.'

'An' wheer's he to come through?' says I.

'Learoyd, my man,' he sings out, 'you're a pretty man av your inches an' a good comrade, but your head is made av duff. Isn't our friend Orth'ris a Taxidermist, an' a rale artist wid his nimble white fingers? An' fwhat's a Taxidermist but a man who can thrate shkins? Do ye mind the white dog that belongs to the Canteen Sargint, bad cess to him – he that's lost half his time an' snarlin' the rest? He shall be lost for *good* now; an' do ye mind that he's the very spit in shape an' size av the Colonel's, barrin' that his tail is an inch too long, an' he has none av the colour that diversifies the rale Rip, an' his timper is that av his masther an' worse? But fwhat is an inch on a dog's tail? An' fwhat to a professional like Orth'ris is a few ringstraked shpots av black, brown, an' white? Nothin' at all, at all.'

Then we meets Orth'ris, an' that little man, bein' sharp as a needle, seed his way through t' business in a minute. An' he went

261

to work a-practisin' 'air-dyes the very next day, beginnin' on some white rabbits he had, an' then he drored all Rip's markins on back of a white Commissariat bullock, so as to get his 'and in an' be sure of his cullers; shadin' off brown into black as nateral as life. If Rip *hed* a fault it was too mich markin', but it was straingely reg'lar, an' Orth'ris settled himself to make a fost-rate job on it when he got haud o' t' Canteen Sargint's dog. Theer niver was sich a dog as thot for bad temper, an' it did nut get no better when his tail hed to be fettled an inch an' a half shorter. But they may talk o' theer Royal Academies as they like. *I* niver seed a bit o' animal paintin' to beat t' copy as Orth'ris made of Rip's marks, wal t' picter itself was snarlin' all t' time an' tryin' to get at Rip standin' theer to be copied as good as goold.

Orth'ris allus hed as mich conceit on himsen as would lift a balloon, an' he wor so pleeased wi' his sham Rip he wor for tekkin' him to Mrs DeSussa before she went awaay. But Mulvaney an' me stopped thot, knowin' Orth'ris's work, though niver so cliver, was nobbut skin-eep.

An' at last Mrs DeSussa fixed t'day for startin' to Munsooree Pahar. We was to tek Rip to t' stayshun i' a basket an' hand him ovver just when they was ready to start, an' then she'd give us t'brass – as was agreed upon.

An' my wod! It were high time she were off, for them 'airdyes upon t'cur's back took a vast of paintin' to keep t'reet culler, tho' Orth'ris spent a matter o' seven rupees six annas i' t' best drooggist shops i' Calcutta.

An' t' Canteen Sargint was lookin' for 'is dog everywheer; an', wi' bein' teed oop, t' beast's timper got waur nor ever.

It wor i' t' evenin' when t' train started thro' Howrah, an' we 'elped Mrs DeSussa wi' about sixty boxes, an' then we gave her t' basket. Orth'ris, for pride iv his work, axed us to let him coom along wi' us, an' he couldn't help liftin' t' lid an' showin' t'cur as he lay coiled oop.

'Oh!' says t'awd lass; 'the beautee! How sweet he looks!' An' just then t' beauty snarled an' showed his teeth, so Mulvaney shuts down t' lid an' says: 'Ye'll be careful, marm, whin ye tek him out. He's disaccustomed to travellin' by t' railway, an' he'll be sure to want his rale mistress an' his friend Learoyd, so ye'll make allowance for his feelings at fost.'

She would do all thot an' more for the dear, good Rip, an' she would nut oppen t' basket till they were miles awaay, for fear onny body should recognise him, an' we were real good and kind soldier-men, we were, an' she honds me a bundle o' notes, an' then cooms oop a few of her relations an' friends to say good-bye – not more than seventy-five there wasn't – an we coots awaay.

What coom to t'three hundred and fifty rupees? Thot's what I can scarcelins tell yo', but we melted it – we melted it. It was share an share alike, for Mulvaney said: 'If Learoyd got hoult av Mrs DeSussa first, sure 'twas I that remimbered the Sargint's dog just in the nick av time, an' Orth'ris was the artist av janius that made a work av art out av that ugly piece av ill-nature. Yet, by way av a thank-offerin' that I was not led into felony by that wicked ould woman, I'll send a thrifle to Father Victor for the poor people he's always beggin' for.'

But me an' Orth'ris, he bein' Cockney an' I bein' pretty far north, did nut see it i' t' saame waay. We'd getten t' brass, an we meaned to keep it. An' soa we did – for a short time.

Noa, noa, we niver heeard a wod more o' t' awd lass. Our Rig'mint went to Pindi, an' t' Canteen Sargint he got himself another tyke instead o' t' one 'at got lost so reg'lar, an' was lost for good at last.

TOOMAI OF THE ELEPHANTS

Kala Nag, which means Black Snake, had served the Indian Government in every way that an elephant could serve it for forty-seven years, and as he was fully twenty years old when he was caught, that makes him nearly seventy – a ripe age for an elephant. He remembered pushing, with a big leather pad on his forehead, at a gun stuck in deep mud, and that was before the Afghan War of 1842, and he had not then come to his full strength. His mother, Radha Pyari – Radha the darling – who had been caught in the same drive with Kala Nag, told him, before his little milk tusks had dropped out, that elephants who were afraid always got hurt; and Kala Nag knew that that advice was good, for the first time that he saw a shell burst he backed, screaming, into a stand of piled rifles, and the bayonets pricked him in all his softest places. So before he was twenty-five he gave up being afraid, and so he was the best-loved and the best-looked-after elephant in the service of the Government of India. He had carried tents, twelve hundred pounds' weight of tents, on the march in Upper India; he had been hoisted into a ship at the end of a steam-crane and taken for days across the water, and made to carry a mortar on his back in a strange and rocky country very far from India, and had seen the Emperor Theodore lying dead in Magdala, and had come back again in the steamer, entitled, so the soldiers said, to the Abyssinian War medal. He had seen his fellow-elephants die of cold and epilepsy and starvation and sunstroke up at a place called Ali Musjid, ten years later; and afterward he had been sent down thousands of miles south to haul and pile big baulks of teak in the timber-yards at Moulmein. There he had half killed an insubordinate young elephant who was shirking his fair share of the work.

After that he was taken off timber-hauling, and employed, with a few score other elephants who were trained to the business, in helping to catch wild elephants among the Garo hills. Elephants are very strictly preserved by the Indian Government. There is one whole department which does nothing else but hunt them, and catch them, and break them in, and send them up and down the country as they are needed for work.

Kala Nag stood ten fair feet at the shoulders, and his tusks had been cut off short at five feet, and bound round the ends, to prevent them splitting, with bands of copper; but he could do more with those stumps than any untrained elephant could do with the real sharpened ones.

When, after weeks and weeks of cautious driving of scattered elephants across the hills, the forty or fifty wild monsters were driven into the last stockade, and the big dropgate, made of tree-trunks lashed together, jarred down behind them, Kala Nag, at the word of command, would go into that flaring, trumpeting pandemonium (generally at night, when the flicker of the torches made it difficult to judge distances), and, picking out the biggest and wildest tusker of the mob, would hammer him and hustle him into quiet while the men on the backs of the other elephants roped and tied the smaller ones.

There was nothing in the way of fighting that Kala Nag, the old wise Black Snake, did not know, for he had stood up more than once in his time to the charge of the wounded tiger, and, curling up his soft trunk to be out of harm's way, had knocked the springing brute sideways in mid-air with a quick sickle-cut of his head, that he had invented all by himself; had knocked him over, and kneeled upon him with his huge knees till the life went out with a gasp and a howl, and there was only a fluffy striped thing on the ground for Kala Nag to pull by the tail.

'Yes,' said Big Toomai, his driver, the son

of Black Toomai who had taken him to Abyssinia, and grandson of Toomai of the Elephants who had seen him caught, 'there is nothing that the Black Snake fears except me. He has seen three generations of us feed him and groom him, and he will live to see four.'

'He is afraid of *me* also,' said Little Toomai, standing up to his full height of four feet, with only one rag upon him. He was ten years old, the eldest son of Big Toomai, and, according to custom, he would take his father's place on Kala Nag's neck when he grew up, and would handle the heavy iron *ankus*, the elephant-goad that had been worn smooth by his father, and his grandfather, and his great-grandfather. He knew what he was talking of; for he had been born under Kala Nag's shadow, had played with the end of his trunk before he could walk, had taken him down to water as soon as he could walk, and Kala Nag would no more have dreamed of disobeying his shrill little orders than he would have dreamed of killing him on that day when Big Toomai carried the little brown baby under Kala Nag's tusks, and told him to salute his master that was to be.

'Yes,' said Little Toomai, 'he is afraid of *me*,' and he took long strides up to Kala Nag, called him a fat old pig, and made him lift up his feet one after the other.

'Wah!' said Little Toomai, 'thou art a big elephant,' and he wagged his fluffy head, quoting his father. 'The Government may pay for elephants, but they belong to us mahouts. When thou art old, Kala Nag, there will come some rich Rajah, and he will buy thee from the Government, on account of thy size and thy manners, and then thou wilt have nothing to do but to carry gold earrings in thy ears, and a gold howdah on thy back, and a red cloth covered with gold on thy sides, and walk at the head of the processions of the king. Then I shall sit on thy neck, O Kala Nag, with a silver *ankus*, and men will run before us with golden sticks, crying, 'Room for the King's elephant!' That will be good, Kala Nag, but not so good as this hunting in the jungles.'

'Umph!' said Big Toomai. 'Thou art a boy, and as wild as a buffalo-calf. This running up and down among the hills is not the best Government service. I am getting old, and I do not love wild elephants. Give me brick elephant-lines, one stall to each elephant, and big stumps to tie them to safely, and flat, broad roads to exercise upon, instead of this come-and-go camping. Aha, the Cawnpore barracks were good. There was a bazaar close by, and only three hours' work a day.'

Little Toomai remembered the Cawnpore elephant-lines and said nothing. He very much preferred the camp life, and hated those broad, flat roads, with the daily grubbing for grass in the forage-reserve, and the long hours when there was nothing to do except to watch Kala Nag fidgeting in his pickets.

What Little Toomai liked was the scramble up bridle-paths that only an elephant could take; the dip into the valley below; the glimpses of the wild elephants browsing miles away; the rush of the frightened pig and peacock under Kala Nag's feet; the blinding warm rains, when all the hills and valleys smoked; the beautiful misty mornings when nobody knew where they would camp that night; the steady, cautious drive of the wild elephants, and the mad rush and blaze and hullabaloo of the last night's drive, when the elephants poured into the stockade like boulders in a landslide, found that they could not get out, and flung themselves at the heavy posts only to be driven back by yells and flaring torches and volleys of blank cartridge.

Even a little boy could be of use there, and Toomai was as useful as three boys. He would get his torch and wave it, and yell with the best. But the really good time came when the driving out began, and the Keddah – that is, the stockade – looked like a picture of the end of the world, and men had to make signs to one another, because they could not hear themselves speak. Then

Little Toomai would climb up to the top of one of the quivering stockade-posts, his sun-bleached brown hair flying loose all over his shoulders, and he looking like a goblin in the torch-light; and as soon as there was a lull you could hear his high-pitched yells of encouragement to Kala Nag, above the trumpeting and crashing, and snapping of ropes, and groans of the tethered elephants. '*Maîl maîl, Kala Nag!* (Go on, go on, Black Snake!) *Dant do!* (Give him the tusk!) *Somalo! Somalo!* (Careful, careful!) *Maro! Mar!* (Hit him, hit him!) Mind the post! *Arre! Arre! Hai! Kya-a-ah!*' he would shout, and the big fight between Kala Nag and the wild elephant would sway to and fro across the Keddah, and the old elephant-catchers would wipe the sweat out of their eyes, and find time to nod to Little Toomai wriggling with joy on the top of the posts.

He did more than wriggle. One night he slid down from the post and slipped in between the elephants, and threw up the loose end of a rope, which had dropped, to a driver who was trying to get a purchase on the leg of a kicking young calf (calves always give more trouble than full-grown animals). Kala Nag saw him, caught him in his trunk, and handed him up to Big Toomai, who slapped him then and there, and put him back on the post.

Next morning he gave him a scolding, and said: 'Are not good brick elephant-lines and a little tent-carrying enough, that thou must needs go elephant-catching on thy own account, little worthless? Now those foolish hunters, whose pay is less than my pay, have spoken to Petersen Sahib of the matter.' Little Toomai was frightened. He did not know much of white men, but Petersen Sahib was the greatest white man in the world to him. He was the head of all the Keddah operations – the man who caught all the elephants for the Government of India, and who knew more about the ways of elephants than any living man.

'What – what will happen?' said Little Toomai.

'Happen! the worst that can happen. Petersen Sahib is a madman. Else why should he go hunting these wild devils? He may even require thee to be an elephant-catcher, to sleep anywhere in these fever-filled jungles, and at last to be trampled to death in the Keddah. It is well that this nonsense ends safely. Next week the catching is over, and we of the plains are sent back to our stations. Then we will march on smooth roads, and forget all this hunting. But, son, I am angry that thou shouldst meddle in the business that belongs to these dirty Assamese jungle-folk. Kala Nag will obey none but me, so I must go with him into the Keddah; but he is only a fighting elephant, and he does not help to rope them. So I sit at my ease, as befits a mahout – not a mere hunter – a mahout, I say, and a man who gets a pension at the end of his service. Is the family of Toomai of the Elephants to be trodden underfoot in the dirt of a Keddah? Bad one! Wicked one! Worthless son! Go and wash Kala Nag and attend to his ears, and see that there are no thorns in his feet; or else Petersen Sahib will surely catch thee and make thee a wild hunter – a follower of elephants' foot-tracks, a jungle-bear. Bah! Shame! Go!'

Little Toomai went off without saying a word, but he told Kala Nag all his grievances while he was examining his feet. 'No matter,' said Little Toomai, turning up the fringe of Kala Nag's huge right ear. 'They have said my name to Petersen Sahib, and perhaps – and perhaps – and perhaps – who knows? Hai! That is a big thorn that I have pulled out!'

The next few days were spent in getting the elephants together, in walking the newly caught wild elephants up and down between a couple of tame ones, to prevent them from giving too much trouble on the downward march to the plains, and in taking stock of the blankets and ropes and things that had been worn out or lost in the forest.

Petersen Sahib came in on his clever she-elephant Pudmini. He had been paying off other camps among the hills, for the season was coming to an end, and there was a native clerk sitting at a table under a tree to pay the drivers their wages. As each man was paid he went back to his elephant, and joined the line that stood ready to start. The catchers, and hunters, and beaters, the men of the regular Keddah, who stayed in the jungle year in and year out, sat on the backs of the elephants that belonged to Petersen Sahib's permanent force, or leaned against the trees with their guns across their arms, and made fun of the drivers who were going away, and laughed when the newly caught elephants broke the line and ran about.

Big Toomai went up to the clerk with Little Toomai behind him, and Machua Appa, the head-tracker, said in an under-tone to a friend of his, 'There goes one piece of good elephant-stuff at least. 'Tis a pity to send that young jungle-cock to moult in the plains.'

Now Petersen Sahib had ears all over him, as a man must have who listens to the most silent of all living things – the wild elephant. He turned where he was lying all along on Pudmini's back, and said, 'What is that? I did not know of a man among the plains-drivers who had wit enough to rope even a dead elephant.'

'This is not a man, but a boy. He went into the Keddah at the last drive, and threw Barmao there the rope when we were trying to get that young calf with the blotch on his shoulder away from his mother.'

Machua Appa pointed at Little Toomai, and Petersen Sahib looked, and Little Toomai bowed to the earth.

'He throw a rope? He is smaller than a picket-pin. Little one, what is thy name?' said Petersen Sahib.

Little Toomai was too frightened to speak, but Kala Nag was behind him, and Toomai made a sign with his hand, and the elephant caught him up in his trunk and held him level with Pudmini's forehead, in front of the great Petersen Sahib. Then Little Toomai covered his face with his hands, for he was only a child, and except where elephants were concerned, he was just as bashful as a child could be.

'Oho!' said Petersen Sahib, smiling underneath his moustache, 'and why didst thou teach thy elephant *that* trick? Was it to help thee steal green corn from the roofs of the houses when the ears are put out to dry?'

'Not green corn, Protector of the Poor – melons,' said Little Toomai, and all the men sitting about broke into a roar of laughter. Most of them had taught their elephants that trick when they were boys. Little

Toomai was hanging eight feet up in the air, and he wished very much that he were eight feet under ground.

'He is Toomai, my son, Sahib,' said Big Toomai, scowling. 'He is a very bad boy, and he will end in a jail, Sahib.'

'Of that I have my doubts,' said Petersen Sahib. 'A boy who can face a full Keddah at his age does not end in jails. See, little one, here are four annas to spend in sweetmeats because thou hast a little head under that great thatch of hair. In time thou mayest become a hunter, too.' Big Toomai scowled more than ever. 'Remember, though, that Keddahs are not good for children to play in,' Petersen Sahib went on.

'Must I never go there, Sahib?' asked Little Toomai, with a big gasp.

'Yes.' Petersen Sahib smiled again. 'When thou hast seen the elephants dance. That is the proper time. Come to me when thou hast seen the elephants dance, and then I will let thee go into all the Keddahs.'

There was another roar of laughter, for that is an old joke among elephant-catchers, and it means just never. There are great cleared flat places hidden away in the forests that are called elephants' ball-rooms, but even these are only found by accident, and no man has ever seen the elephants dance. When a driver boasts of his skill and bravery the other drivers say, 'And when didst *thou* see the elephants dance?'

Kala Nag put Little Toomai down, and he bowed to the earth again and went away with his father, and gave the silver four-anna piece to his mother, who was nursing his baby-brother, and they all were put upon Kala Nag's back, and the line of grunting, squealing elephants rolled down the hill-path to the plains. It was a very lively march on account of the new elephants, who gave trouble at every ford, and who needed coaxing or beating every other minute.

Big Toomai prodded Kala Nag spitefully, for he was very angry, but Little Toomai was too happy to speak. Petersen Sahib had noticed him, and given him money, so he felt as a private soldier would feel if he had been called out of the ranks and praised by his commander-in-chief.

'What did Petersen Sahib mean by the elephant-dance?' he said, at last, softly to his mother.

Big Toomai heard him and grunted. 'That thou shouldst never be one of these hill-buffaloes of trackers. *That* was what he meant. Oh, you in front, what is blocking the way?'

An Assamese driver, two or three elephants ahead, turned round angrily, crying: 'Bring up Kala Nag, and knock this youngster of mine into good behaviour. Why should Petersen Sahib have chosen *me* to go down with you donkeys of the ricefields? Lay your beast alongside, Toomai, and let him prod with his tusks. By all the Gods of the Hills, these new elephants are possessed, or else they can smell their companions in the jungle.'

Kala Nag hit the new elephant in the ribs and knocked the wind out of him, as Big Toomai said, 'We have swept the hills of wild elephants at the last catch. It is only your carelessness in driving. Must I keep order along the whole line?'

'Hear him!' said the other driver. '"*We* have swept the hills!" Ho! ho! You are very wise, you plains-people. Any one but a mud-head who never saw the jungle would know that *they* know that the drives are ended for the season. Therefore all the wild elephants to-night will – but why should I waste wisdom on a river-turtle?'

'What will they do?' Little Toomai called out.

'*Ohé*, little one. Art thou there? Well, I will tell thee, for thou hast a cool head. They will dance, and it behoves thy father, who has swept *all* the hills of *all* the elephants, to double-chain his pickets to-night.'

'What talk is this?' said Big Toomai. 'For forty years, father and son, we have tended elephants, and we have never heard such moonshine about dances.'

'Yes; but a plains-man who lives in a hut

knows only the four walls of his hut. Well, leave thy elephants unshackled tonight and see what comes; as for their dancing, I have seen the place where – *Bapree-Bap!* how many windings has the Dihang River? Here is another ford, and we must swim the calves. Stop still, you behind there.'

And in this way, talking and wrangling and splashing through the rivers, they made their first march to a sort of receiving-camp for the new elephants; but they lost their tempers long before they got there.

Then the elephants were chained by their hind legs to their big stumps of pickets, and extra ropes were fitted to the new elephants, and the fodder was piled before them, and the hilldrivers went back to Petersen Sahib through the afternoon light, telling the plains-drivers to be extra careful that night, and laughing when the plains-drivers asked the reason.

Little Toomai attended to Kala Nag's supper, and as evening fell wandered through the camp, unspeakably happy, in search of a tom-tom. When an Indian child's heart is full, he does not run about and make a noise in an irregular fashion. He sits down to a sort of revel all by himself. And Little Toomai had been spoken to by Petersen Sahib! If he had not found what he wanted I believe he would have burst. But the sweetmeat-seller in the camp lent him a little tom-tom – a drum beaten with the flat of the hand – and he sat down, cross-legged before Kala Nag as the stars began to come out, the tom-tom in his lap, and he thumped and he thumped and he thumped, and the more he thought of the great honour that had been done to him, the more he thumped, all alone among the elephant-fodder. There was no tune and no words, but the thumping made him happy.

The new elephants strained at their ropes, and squealed and trumpeted from time to time, and he could hear his mother in the camp hut putting his small brother to sleep with an old, old song about the great God Shiv, who once told all the animals what they should eat. It is a very soothing lullaby, and the first verse says:

Shiv, who poured the harvest and made
    the winds to blow,
Sitting at the doorways of a day of long
    ago,
Gave to each his portion, food and toil
    and fate,
From the King upon the *guddee* to the
    Beggar at the gate.
All things made he – Shiva the Preserver.
Mahadeo! Mahadeo! He made all –
Thorn for the camel, fodder for the kine,
And mother's heart for sleepy head, O
    little son of mine!

Little Toomai came in with a joyous *tunk-a-tunk* at the end of each verse, till he felt sleepy and stretched himself on the fodder at Kala Nag's side.

At last the elephants began to lie down one after another, as is their custom, till only Kala Nag at the right of the line was left standing up; and he rocked slowly from side to side, his ears put forward to listen to the night wind as it blew very slowly across the hills. The air was full of all the night noises that, taken together, make one big silence – the click of one bamboo-stem against the other, the rustle of something alive in the undergrowth, the scratch and squawk of a half-waked bird (birds are awake in the night much more often than we imagine), and the fall of water ever so far away. Little Toomai slept for some time, and when he waked it was brilliant moonlight, and Kala Nag was still standing up with his ears cocked. Little Toomai turned, rustling in the fodder, and watched the curve of his big back against half the stars in heaven; and while he watched he heard, so far away that it sounded no more than a pinhole of noise pricked through the stillness, the 'hoot-toot' of a wild elephant.

All the elephants in the lines jumped up as if they had been shot, and their grunts at last waked the sleeping mahouts, and they came out and drove in the picket-pegs with big mallets, and tightened this rope and knotted that till all was quiet. One new elephant had nearly grubbed up his picket, and Big Toomai took off Kala Nag's leg-chain and shackled that elephant fore-foot to hind-foot, but slipped a loop of grass-string round Kala Nag's leg, and told him to remember that he was tied fast. He knew that he and his father and his grandfather had done the very same thing hundreds of times before. Kala Nag did not answer to the order by gurgling, as he usually did. He stood still, looking out across the moonlight, his head a little raised, and his ears spread like fans, up to the great folds of the Garo hills.

'Look to him if he grows restless in the night,' said Big Toomai to Little Toomai, and he went into the hut and slept. Little Toomai was just going to sleep, too, when he heard the coir string snap with a little 'tang,' and Kala Nag rolled out of his pickets as slowly and as silently as a cloud rolls out of the mouth of a valley. Little Toomai pattered after him, barefooted, down the road in the moonlight, calling under his breath, 'Kala Nag! Kala Nag! Take me with you, O Kala Nag!' The elephant turned without a sound, took three strides back to the boy in the moonlight, put down his trunk, swung him up to his neck, and almost before Little Toomai had settled his knees, slipped into the forest.

There was one blast of furious trumpeting from the lines, and then the silence shut down on everything, and Kala Nag began to move. Sometimes a tuft of high grass washed along his sides as a wave washes along the sides of a ship, and sometimes a cluster of wild-pepper vines would scrape along his back, or a bamboo would creak where his shoulder touched it; but between those times he moved absolutely without any sound, drifting through the thick Garo forest as though it had been smoke. He was going uphill, but though Little Toomai watched the stars in the rifts of the trees, he could not tell in what direction.

Then Kala Nag reached the crest of the ascent and stopped for a minute, and Little Toomai could see the tops of the trees lying all speckled and furry under the moonlight for miles and miles, and the blue-white mist over the river in the hollow. Toomai leaned forward and looked, and he felt that the forest was awake below him – awake and alive and crowded. A big brown fruit-eating bat brushed past his ear; a porcupine's quills rattled in the thicket; and in the darkness between the tree-stems he heard a hog-bear digging hard in the moist, warm earth, and snuffing as it digged.

Then the branches closed over his head

again, and Kala Nag began to go down into the valley – not quietly this time, but as a runaway gun goes down a steep bank – in one rush. The huge limbs moved as steadily as pistons, eight feet to each stride, and the wrinkled skin of the elbow-points rustled. The undergrowth on either side of him ripped with a noise like torn canvas, and the saplings that he heaved away right and left with his shoulders sprang back again, and banged him on the flank, and great trails of creepers, all matted together, hung from his tusks as he threw his head from side to side and ploughed out his pathway. Then Little Toomai laid himself down close to the great neck, lest a swinging bough should sweep him to the ground, and he wished that he were back in the lines again.

The grass began to get squashy, and Kala Nag's feet sucked and squelched as he put them down, and the night mist at the bottom of the valley chilled Little Toomai. There was a splash and a trample, and the rush of running water, and Kala Nag strode through the bed of a river, feeling his way at each step. Above the noise of the water, as it swirled round the elephant's legs, Little Toomai could hear more splashing and some trumpeting both up stream and down – great grunts and angry snortings, and all the mist about him seemed to be full of rolling, wavy shadows.

'*Ai!*' he said, half aloud, his teeth chattering. 'The elephant-folk are out to-night. It *is* the dance, then.'

Kala Nag swashed out of the water, blew his trunk clear, and began another climb; but this time he was not alone, and he had not to make his path. That was made already, six feet wide, in front of him, where the bent jungle-grass was trying to recover itself and stand up. Many elephants must have gone that way only a few minutes before. Little Toomai looked back, and behind him a great wild tusker, with his little pig's eyes glowing like hot coals, was just lifting himself out of the misty river. Then the trees closed up again, and they went on and up, with trumpetings and crashings, and the sound of breaking branches on every side of them.

At last Kala Nag stood still between two tree-trunks at the very top of the hill. They were part of a circle of trees that grew round an irregular space of some three or four acres, and in all that space, as Little Toomai could see, the ground had been trampled down as hard as a brick floor. Some trees grew in the centre of the clearing, but their bark was rubbed away, and the white wood beneath showed all shiny and polished in the patches of moonlight. There were creepers hanging from the upper branches, and the bells of the flowers of the creepers, great waxy white things like convolvuluses, hung down fast asleep; but within the limits of the clearing there was not a single blade of green – nothing but the trampled earth.

The moonlight showed it all iron-grey, except where some elephants stood upon it, and their shadows were inky black. Little Toomai looked, holding his breath, with his eyes starting out of his head, and as he looked, more and more and more elephants swung out into the open from between the tree-trunks. Little Toomai could count only up to ten, and he counted again and again on his fingers till he lost count of the tens, and his head began to swim. Outside the clearing he could hear them crashing in the undergrowth as they worked their way up the hillside; but as soon as they were within the circle of the tree-trunks they moved like ghosts.

There were white-tusked wild males, with fallen leaves and nuts and twigs lying in the wrinkles of their necks and the folds of their ears; fat, slow-footed she-elephants, with restless little pinky-black calves only three or four feet high running under their stomachs; young elephants with their tusks just beginning to show, and very proud of them; lanky, scraggy old-maid elephants, with their hollow, anxious faces, and trunks like rough bark; savage old bull-elephants, scarred from shoulder to flank with great weals and cuts of bygone fights, and the caked dirt of their solitary mud-baths dropping from their shoulders; and there was one with a broken tusk and the marks of the full-stroke, the terrible drawing scrape, of a tiger's claws on his side.

They were standing head to head, or walking to and fro across the ground in couples, or rocking and swaying all by themselves – scores and scores of elephants.

Toomai knew that, so long as he lay still on Kala Nag's neck, nothing would happen to him; for even in the rush and scramble of a Keddah-drive a wild elephant does not reach up with his trunk and drag a man off the neck of a tame elephant; and these elephants were not thinking of men that night. Once they started and put their ears forward when they heard the chinking of a leg-iron in the forest, but it was Pudmini, Petersen Sahib's pet elephant, her chain snapped short off, grunting, snuffling up the hillside. She must have broken her pickets, and come straight from Petersen Sahib's camp; and Little Toomai saw another elephant, one that he did not know, with deep rope-galls on his back and breast. He, too, must have run away from some camp in the hills about.

At last there was no sound of any more elephants moving in the forest, and Kala Nag rolled out from his station between the trees and went into the middle of the crowd, clucking and gurgling, and all the elephants began to talk in their own tongue, and to move about.

Still lying down, Little Toomai looked down upon scores and scores of broad backs, and wagging ears, and tossing trunks, and little rolling eyes. He heard the click of tusks as they crossed other tusks by accident, and the dry rustle of trunks twined together, and the chafing of enormous sides and shoulders in the crowd, and the incessant flick and *hissh* of the great tails.

Then a cloud came over the moon, and he sat in black darkness; but the quiet, steady hustling and pushing and gurgling went on just the same. He knew that there were elephants all round Kala Nag, and that there was no chance of backing him out of the assembly; so he set his teeth and shivered. In a Keddah at least there was torch-light and shouting, but here he was all alone in the dark, and once a trunk came up and touched him on the knee.

Then an elephant trumpeted, and they all took it up for five or ten terrible seconds. The dew from the trees above spattered down like rain on the unseen backs, and a dull booming noise began, not very loud at first, and Little Toomai could not tell what it was; but it grew and grew, and Kala Nag lifted up one fore foot and then the other, and brought them down on the ground – one-two, one-two, as steadily as trip-hammers. The elephants were stamping all together now, and it sounded like a war-drum beaten at the mouth of a cave. The dew fell from the trees till there was no more left to fall, and the booming went on, and the ground rocked and shivered, and Little Toomai put his hands up to his ears to shut out the sound. But it was all one gigantic jar that ran through him – this stamp of hundreds of heavy feet on the raw earth. Once or twice he could feel Kala Nag and all the others surge forward a few strides, and the thumping would change to the crushing sound of juicy green things being bruised, but in a minute or two the boom of feet on hard earth began again. A tree was creaking and groaning somewhere near him. He put out his arm and felt the bark, but Kala Nag moved forward, still tramping, and he could not tell where he was in the clearing. There was no sound from the elephants, except once, when two or three little calves squeaked together. Then he heard a thump and a shuffle, and the booming went on. It must have lasted fully two hours, and Little Toomai ached in every nerve; but he knew by the smell of the night air that the dawn was coming.

The morning broke in one sheet of pale yellow behind the green hills, and the booming stopped with the first ray, as though the light had been an order. Before Little Toomai had got the ringing out of his head, before even he had shifted his position, there was not an elephant in sight except Kala Nag, Pudmini, and the elephant with the rope-galls, and there was neither sign nor rustle nor whisper down the hillsides to show where the others had gone.

Little Toomai stared again and again. The clearing, as he remembered it, had grown in the night. More trees stood in the middle of it, but the undergrowth and the jungle-grass at the sides had been rolled back. Little Toomai stared once more. Now he understood the trampling. The elephants had stamped out more room – had stamped the thick grass and juicy cane to trash, the trash into slivers, the slivers into tiny fibres, and the fibres into hard earth.

'Wah!' said Little Toomai, and his eyes were very heavy. 'Kala Nag, my lord, let us keep by Pudmini and go to Petersen Sahib's camp, or I shall drop from thy neck.'

The third elephant watched the two go away, snorted, wheeled round, and took his own path. He may have belonged to some little native king's establishment, fifty or sixty or a hundred miles away.

Two hours later, as Petersen Sahib was eating early breakfast, the elephants, who had been double-chained that night, began to trumpet, and Pudmini, mired to the shoulders, with Kala Nag, very foot-sore, shambled into the camp.

Little Toomai's face was grey and pinched, and his hair was full of leaves and drenched with dew; but he tried to salute Petersen Sahib, and cried faintly: 'The dance – the elephant-dance! I have seen it, and – I die!' As Kala Nag sat down, he slid off his neck in a dead faint.

But, since native children have no nerves worth speaking of, in two hours he was lying very contentedly in Petersen Sahib's hammock with Petersen Sahib's shooting-coat under his head, and a glass of warm milk, a little brandy, with a dash of quinine inside of him; and while the old hairy, scarred hunters of the jungles sat three-deep before him, looking at him as though he were a spirit, he told his tale in short words, as a child will, and wound up with:

'Now, if I lie in one word, send men to see, and they will find that the elephant-folk have trampled down more room in their dance-room, and they will find ten and ten, and many times ten, tracks leading to that dance-room. They made more room with their feet. I have seen it. Kala Nag took me, and I saw. Also Kala Nag is very leg-weary!'

Little Toomai lay back and slept all through the long afternoon and into the twilight, and while he slept Petersen Sahib and Machua Appa followed the track of the two elephants for fifteen miles across the hills. Petersen Sahib had spent eighteen years in catching elephants, and he had only once before found such a dance-place. Machua Appa had no need to look twice at the clearing to see what had been done there, or to scratch with his toe in the packed, rammed earth.

'The child speaks truth,' said he. 'All this was done last night, and I have counted seventy tracks crossing the river. See, Sahib, where Pudmini's leg-iron cut the bark off that tree! Yes; she was there too.'

They looked at each other, and up and down, and they wondered; for the ways of elephants are beyond the wit of any man, black or white, to fathom.

'Forty years and five,' said Machua Appa, 'have I followed my lord the elephant, but never have I heard that any child of man had seen what this child has seen. By all the Gods of the Hills, it is – what can we say?' and he shook his head.

When they got back to camp it was time for the evening meal. Petersen Sahib ate alone in his tent, but he gave orders that the camp should have two sheep and some fowls, as well as a double ration of flour and rice and salt, for he knew that there would be a feast.

Big Toomai had come up hot-foot from the camp in the plains to search for his son and his elephant, and now that he had found them he looked at them as though he were afraid of them both. And there was a feast by the blazing camp-fires in front of the lines of picketed elephants, and Little Toomai was the hero of it all; and the big brown elephant-catchers, the trackers and drivers and ropers, and the men who know all the secrets of breaking the wildest elephants, passed him from one to the other, and they marked his forehead with blood from the breast of a newly killed jungle-cock, to show that he was a forester, initiated and free of all the jungles.

And at last, when the flames died down, and the red light of the logs made the elephants look as though they had been dipped in blood too, Machua Appa, the head of all the drivers of all the Keddahs – Machua Appa, Petersen Sahib's other self, who had never seen a made road in forty years: Machua Appa, who was so great that he had no other name than Machua Appa – leaped to his feet, with Little Toomai held high in the air above his head, and shouted:

'Listen, my brothers. Listen, too, you my lords in the lines there, for I, Machua Appa, am speaking! This little one shall no more be called Little Toomai, but Toomai of the Elephants, as his great-grandfather was called before him. What never man has seen he has seen through the long night, and the favour of the elephant-folk and of the Gods of the Jungles is with him. He shall become a great tracker; he shall become greater than I, even I – Machua Appa! He shall follow the new trail, and the stale trail, and the mixed trail, with a clear eye! He shall take no harm in the Keddah when he runs under their bellies to rope the wild tuskers; and if he slips before the feet of the charging bull-elephant, that bull-elephant shall know who he is and shall not crush him. *Aihai!* my lords in the chains,' – he whirled up the line of pickets – 'here is the little one that has seen your dances in your hidden places – the sight that never man saw! Give him honour, my lords! *Salaam karo*, my children. Make your salute to Toomai of the Elephants! Gunga Pershad, ahaa! Hira Guj, Birchi Guj, Kuttar Guj, ahaa! Pudmini – thou hast seen him at the dance, and thou too, Kala Nag, my pearl among elephants! – ahaa! Together! To Toomai of the Elephants. *Barrao!*'

And at that last wild yell the whole line flung up their trunks till the tips touched their foreheads, and broke out into the full salute, the crashing trumpet-peal that only the Viceroy of India hears – the Salaamut of the Keddah.

But it was all for the sake of Little Toomai,

who had seen what never man had seen before – the dance of the elephants at night and alone in the heart of the Garo hills!

PARADE-SONG
OF THE
CAMP-ANIMALS

ELEPHANTS OF THE GUN-TEAMS

We lent to Alexander the strength of
  Hercules,
The wisdom of our foreheads, the cunning
  of our knees;
We bowed our necks to service; they ne'er
  were loosed again –
Make way there, way for the ten-foot
  teams
  Of the Forty-Pounder train!

GUN-BULLOCKS

Those heroes in their harnesses avoid a
  cannon-ball,
And what they know of powder upsets
  them one and all;
Then *we* come into action and tug the
  guns again, –
Make way there, way for the twenty-yoke
  Of the Forty-Pounder train!

CAVALRY HORSES

By the brand on my withers, the finest of
  tunes

Is played by the Lancers, Hussars, and
  Dragoons,
And it's sweeter than 'Stables' or 'Water'
  to me,
The Cavalry Canter of Bonnie Dundee'!

Then feed us and break us and handle and
  groom,
And give us good riders and plenty of
  room,
And launch us in column of squadron and
  see
The way of the war-horse to 'Bonnie
  Dundee'!

SCREW-GUN MULES

As me and my companions were
  scrambling up a hill,
The path was lost in rolling stones, but we
  went forward still;
For we can wriggle and climb, my lads,
  and turn up everywhere,
And it's our delight on a mountain height,
  with a leg or two to spare!

Good luck to every sergeant, then, that
  lets us pick our road!
Bad luck to all the driver-men that cannot
  pack a load!
For we can wriggle and climb, my lads,
  and turn up everywhere,
And it's our delight on a mountain height,

with a leg or two to spare!

COMMISSARIAT CAMELS
We haven't a camelty tune of our own
To help us trollop along,
But every neck is a hair-trombone
(*Rtt-ta-ta-ta!* is a hair-trombone!)
And this is our marching-song:
Can't! Don't! Shan't! Won't!
Pass it along the line!
Somebody's pack has slid from his back,
'Wish it were only mine!
Somebody's load has tipped off in the
  road –
Cheer for a halt and a row!
Urrr! Yarrh! Grr! Arrh!
Somebody's catching it now!

ALL THE BEASTS TOGETHER
Children of the Camp are we,
Serving each in his degree;
Children of the yoke and goad,
Pack and harness, pad and load.
See our line across the plain,
Like a heel-rope bent again,
Reaching, writhing, rolling far,
Sweeping all away to war!
While the men that walk beside,
Dusty, silent, heavy-eyed,
Cannot tell why we or they
March and suffer day by day.
  Children of the Camp are we,

Serving each in his degree;
Children of the yoke and goad,
Pack and harness, pad and load.

The publishers hope that this book has given you enjoyable reading. Large Print Books are especially designed to be as easy to see and hold as possible. If you wish a complete list of our books please ask at your local library or write directly to:

Dales Large Print Books
Magna House, Long Preston,
Skipton, North Yorkshire.
BD23 4ND

This Large Print Book, for people
who cannot read normal print,
is published under the auspices of

THE ULVERSCROFT FOUNDATION